chronicles of the
unexplained

GARY GILLESPIE

chronicles of the
unexplained

**True Stories of Haunted Houses,
Bigfoot & Other Paranormal Encounters**

Llewellyn Publications
Woodbury, Minnesota

FIRST EDITION
First Printing, 2015

Cover art: Shutterstock/94230298/©isoga
Cover design: Kevin R. Brown
Editing: Jennifer Ackman

Llewellyn Publications is a registered trademark of Llewellyn Worldwide Ltd.

Library of Congress Cataloging-in-Publication Data

Gillespie, Gary, 1966–
  Chronicles of the unexplained : true stories of haunted houses, bigfoot & other paranormal encounters / by Gary Gillespie. — First edition.
      pages cm
   ISBN 978-0-7387-4538-1
1. Haunted places. 2. Monsters. I. Title.
   BF1461.G57 2015
   001.94—dc23
                        2015003844

Llewellyn Publications
A Division of Llewellyn Worldwide, Ltd.
2143 Wooddale Drive
Woodbury, MN 55125-2989
www.llewellyn.com

Printed in the United States of America

Contents

Foreword

I first learned of Gary Gillespie and his ability to tell a story back in 2011 when I was collecting true accounts of haunted highway encounters for my book *Trucker Ghost Stories*. I had cast a wide net in my search appearing on trucker and paranormal radio shows and podcasts, posting calls for stories on the online trucker's forums and websites, and contacting trucker friends and prominent people in the trucking industry. I even brought fliers about my book to the "World's Largest Truck Stop," Iowa 80, in Walcott, Iowa.

I was looking for the best and most bizarre stories of encounters with the inhabitants of otherworldly realms from truckers and those affiliated with the trucking industry. What I heard—from scores of hardworking, down-to-earth people who didn't even believe in such things until they actually encountered them—were sincere accounts of run-ins with a terrifying cast of astral-realm denizens and anomalies, from screaming ghosts and howling demons, to predatory monsters, shadow people, goat-footed hitchhikers, Bigfoot, aliens, phantom vehicles, and sinister roads leading to nowhere.

At the time, Gary was the Colorado trucking industry columnist for the online magazine, *Examiner.com*. He had written a special Halloween-themed column that included three incredible, true ghost stories involving trucks and truck drivers; all of which made it into my book. (The stories are of a haunted truck with a mission, a mysterious Mack truck that may itself have been a ghost, and an OTR driver's threatening, up-close-and-personal encounter with an elusive creature that, officially at least, doesn't exist.)

When I wrote to Gary to ask permission to include his stories in my book, I told him he was a natural storyteller with a great writing voice. He told me he was thinking about writing a book. I said, "You should," and we've kept in touch ever since. Gary graciously appeared with me on *Darkness Radio* to promote *Trucker Ghost Stories,* and has been willing to do whatever is needed to help get the word out about my book.

In this fine collection of very odd and spooky stories, you'll find ghost stories from the road, from Midwestern rail yards, and from the man camps and oilfields of North Dakota. There are stories of eerie, bone-chilling encounters while hunting, camping, and four-wheeling. These true stories encompass everything from run-ins with skinwalkers to very haunted houses, animal mutilations, Bigfoot, unhappy ghosts, and dark entities. One of my favorite stories—because it is so very strange and ominous—tells of a silent, haunted piece of land with the terrifying ability to "take" things and make them disappear forever. This collection also includes very moving stories of spirits coming back to offer protection, assistance, and gratitude to those who helped them in life.

I have the highest regard for Gary and I'm a big fan of his writing. It's clear that he is dedicated to his family and his work, has a true appreciation of history, and possesses an engaging sense of humor about life's challenges and mysteries. I particularly like his passionate descriptions of the land and times past. Credible, generous-spirited, and down-to-earth, Gary brings a strong human element to his writing, making him a perfect guide to the world of the weird and unexplained.

I have thoroughly enjoyed reading Gary's book (and hearing about some of these stories as he was living them). I know paranormal fans will be entertained, happily frightened, and even inspired by the stories in *Chronicles of the Unexplained*.

—Annie Wilder, author of
The House of Spirits and Whispers,
Spirits Out of Time,
and *Trucker Ghost Stories*

Introduction

I have had the pleasure of having jobs in many varying industries, which has taken me to every corner of our beautiful country. Through my travels I was able to meet wonderful people in every location I went. It was very strange how people would come to me with some very interesting stories about paranormal and supernatural experiences. It seemed as though whatever was compelling me to write a book of this nature was not going to let me rest until I did it.

My jobs have included everything from trucking to welding in the oilfield. Considering the type of people I usually worked with and the stereotypes that go along with these industries, most would think it would be impossible to bring up and talk about these subjects. Surprisingly, I have found the opposite to be true. Many of the accounts in this book have happened recently and may even provide some insight into what messages are coming from the other side, and why they are so desperate for us to hear those messages.

Most of these stories are regional with Colorado, North Dakota, Wyoming, Nebraska, and my childhood home of Iowa all represented here. Although these are the only locations that have been included here, as you read remember that these things can happen anywhere. It may even be happening in your backyard.

The following pages include real accounts of events that happened to real people, in real houses, in real families. Some of the accounts are definitely strange, but still relatively harmless. Others are not so harmless. They include death, a breakdown in personal health, and financial ruin with no reasonable explanations as to how it all happened. Even medical doctors couldn't explain what happened!

The worst of these stories occurred to my family and me. It is most likely one of the biggest reasons I started to research these subjects and the need to find a reason for what happened, and why I wanted to write this book.

It has been quite a journey, and I am glad you have chosen to experience some of it with me.

chapter one

Haunted Houses

Not all haunted houses are dilapidated, old houses on the hill surrounded by dead trees. Some could be right next door. That includes houses in new developments, well-kept houses with beautifully manicured lawns, or the rental home that can never stay rented for very long. If there was a way to identify the most notoriously haunted houses, it would be shocking to see how such an ordinary-looking place could be haunted. It doesn't even take a death on the premises to cause it to be haunted. In some cases, the very land on which the home was built could be cursed, or be a location that seems to attract evil.

When you start to search for your dream home and begin talking to your realtor, or if you are starting to research your next remodel project, please be sure and listen to your innermost feelings more than the marketing advice from a real estate agent or contractor. It could be the best thing you could ever do for you and your family's well-being.

Don't be afraid ... It's only a Demon

For our family, my job transfer to western Colorado was an exciting, new adventure. During the first few months I was by myself and lived in a camper that I pulled behind my truck. I spent a great deal of time camping at the Colorado National Monument and would explore other areas of the park, I also rested and concentrated on looking for a house on the weekends. I had hoped that as soon as I found a house and was settled, they would have taken care of everything in the old house and be able to move out to me. I looked at a number of houses, but I kept coming back to one house in the Redlands. I loved the area, absolutely loved the big yards, and I particularly loved the fact that the property had ditch water, which I planned to use to irrigate the gardens I wanted to develop. The choice was narrowed down to a cute little fixer-upper in the Redlands or a comparably priced newer home on the south side of town. I eventually chose the fixer-upper and purchased it for way below the asking price. This was lucky, and necessary, because of all the work that needed to be done. I was happy with the decision.

It was a brick ranch home that had lots of windows and a garage that I was hoping to convert into my wood shop that I would use for furniture building and the remodel that I wanted to do myself. The home had oak hardwood floors throughout, which I would sand and refinish. Other than that, I planned to update everything else in the house as time went on. In hindsight, I should have suspected something was wrong when I told the sellers they could take their time moving out. They still had a lot of items in the house and it would be at least two weeks before my family was able to make the move from our old house. The sellers insisted they would be out that evening, and they were. They wasted no time in removing all their effects from that house. Being that the house was empty, and officially mine, I moved the mattress from my camper to the master bedroom and began sleeping there.

All of our furniture and supplies were still with my family, so I stocked the kitchen with some basics, installed a radio in the kitchen so I could have some music, and began making plans for my family's arrival in a few weeks. I worked the graveyard shift so I would leave the house around ten p.m., and worked as much overtime as I could, so I mostly just slept when I was at the house. I didn't notice anything out of the ordinary with the house other than it occasionally sounded like doors were opening and closing. I was alone in the house and I knew it wasn't anyone else, so I assumed it was probably just the neighbors. I later realized you couldn't hear much of anything outside of the house because of the brick walls, so that ruled out the neighbors. I didn't think much about what the cause of the noise was, but it kept waking me up and I already wasn't sleeping very well in the new house.

My family finally arrived at the end of July. As with any move, the kids were very excited and most concerned about picking out their rooms. After the rooms had been settled, we began the daunting task of unloading the U-Haul and cars, and putting the boxes and furniture into their respective rooms. My wife and I slept in the living room that first night and the kids slept on their mattresses in their new rooms.

We made it through the night with nothing happening, but the following morning my daughter woke up laughing and said, "Alright, who did it?" Not knowing what she was talking about, my wife walked into her room and saw that all of her toy horses, at least twenty of them, were placed on the floor surrounding her mattress with their faces pointed toward the bed. My wife thought that maybe my daughter did it late at night and forgot about it, but she swore she didn't do it. She hadn't even had time to unpack them yet, so whoever had done this had unpacked them and then placed them around her bed. After the first night, our life at our new house was fairly quiet for a few weeks aside from the occasional footsteps on the wood floors that we foolishly brushed off as nothing or that we were just hearing things.

One of my daughter's new friends had informed her that the original owner of the house had died in the master bedroom about four years earlier of an apparent heart attack, but none of us gave it any thought. I was way too busy at work for that kind of nonsense. We probably should have paid more attention to her friend.

As they usually do, the remodeling project was taking much longer than I wanted it to. I started in my son's room and we found a bunch of children's books that were aimed toward girls hidden in the walls. One of them had a note that welcomed someone into the family, so we wondered if a young girl had been adopted into a family or moved in with the family due to other circumstances. We all thought it was very strange that the books would be in the walls, no matter what the situation.

Things really started to happen when I finished my son's room and was getting ready to start the family room and office. My wife and I were still sleeping on a bed in the living room because I had been so focused on the other rooms that I hadn't gotten to ours yet. It was one of those rare nights when I allowed our Australian Shepherd, Violet, to sleep in between us. If you have ever slept with a dog, you know how little sleep you actually get when a dog is in your bed. On top of everything else, my sleeping habits hadn't improved at all since I had moved in.

We had an oscillating fan running at the foot of the bed because my only hope for any sleep at all in this house was when I had a fan running to create white noise. Otherwise, noises were constantly waking me up. On this particular night, I was startled awake when I heard a strange rattling noise coming from the fan. I drowsily looked to the foot of the bed to check on it, but it looked okay so I lay back down. Just as my head hit the pillow, I heard it again. This time the dog looked up too, and I noticed that the fan seemed to be closer to the bed, but again, I didn't give it much thought because I was just too tired. Within a few minutes the fan was right against the bed, and part of our sheet had been pulled into the fan and stopped the blades from turning.

I jumped out of bed and said, "What the hell is going on?" The fan had moved closer to the bed, so that meant it was moving *against* the wind blowing from it. Besides that, it had sticky, rubber feet on the base so that it wouldn't be able to slide along the wood floor. I pulled the fan away from the bed, put a doorstop against it to make sure it couldn't move, and lay down again. The dog seemed confused but didn't seem alarmed.

I had just started to doze off when, over the sound of the fan, I heard a loud, kissing sound that sounded as if someone was calling my dog. She bolted upright, was wide-awake with her ears straight up, and was looking into the dark kitchen where it sounded like the noise was coming from. It was two a.m. and I checked the house, but everyone was asleep. This time Violet seemed a little upset, but would not leave the bed; it was as if she was protecting us. After going through the whole house I, of course, came up with nothing, so I went back to bed a little more uneasy than before.

During our second year in the house more things started happening in my daughter's room. She had her own television that would turn on and off by itself, DVDs would start to play at all hours of the day, books would continually fall off of the bookshelves, and her bedroom lights would turn on and off. We started to notice that if our daughter was gone overnight for any reason, such as a sleepover at a friends' house, the fire alarm would go off in her room at exactly two a.m. every time, without fail.

My daughter soon realized that there was something wrong in the house, but I tried to reason things out. Being in my forties, I thought I had outgrown the ghost thing. Apparently, you can't outgrow it. If my daughter, who was only fourteen at the time, had days off from school and was home alone, the house became much more active. Doors would open and close, something would scratch very loudly at the front door, and all the cabinets would open when she walked into the kitchen. The phone calls to my wife at work were almost constant because my daughter was becoming quite scared of the house and didn't want to be there alone.

My daughter had a very disturbing dream while sleeping in her room one night. She dreamt of a young girl with long hair who would pace back and forth outside of her bedroom window, occasionally stopping to look in at her. According to my daughter, given this girl's stringy hair, gray skin, and white eyes, we concluded that the girl in the dream was obviously dead. It was one of those dreams that was very real and you seem to never forget. Shortly after that dream, a box of my daughter's toys came up missing and was never found. We don't know if the dream and the missing toys are related, but it seemed pretty suspicious to us that they both happened around the same time.

Suddenly, my health started to become a problem. Part of the difficulty was that I couldn't sleep well in the house. When work would sometimes take me out into the field, I would get my most restful sleep in the cab of a truck hours away from the house. I started having severe panic attacks that closely resembled a heart attack. I went to the emergency room on three separate occasions because I couldn't breathe and thought I was having a heart attack. The worst was when my blood pressure was 181/118. I drove myself to the hospital and went straight to cardiac care, but my blood pressure went back down to normal, all the tests came back normal, and re-vealed nothing abnormal.

We started going to a new physician, and after talking to me for about an hour and checking me out, she asked me about stress. She was religious, so I think that she may have been on to something. She suggested I seek help through my church, which is normally very out of bounds advice for a doctor to give to their patients, but I later found out she could sense that something very bad was surrounding me and my family. She wanted to help, but she wasn't sure how and couldn't come right out and say it.

I eventually hired a new employee who had lost his hous-ing arrangement. In a town with oilfield workers, this could mean being homeless because it can take weeks for a rental to open up, and that's only if you can afford it. I told him he could stay in our office since we had a hide-a-bed in there that we weren't using, as well as the computer and desk. Af-ter about three days, he began to mention that he couldn't sleep worth a damn in that room.

I asked him why and he replied, "Dude, you got a god-damned ghost or something in this place." I laughed because he had a real strong southern accent and it sounded funny. I asked him why he thought the place was haunted and he said that the computer turns on, logs on to Windows, and starts searching. That night I put a surge protector on the computer and turned it off before he got home from work.

The next morning I asked if the computer turned on last night and he said, "Yep, it sure did. At two a.m., as usual."

I thought he was pulling my leg to get me back for scaring him at work a few days before. I guess he wasn't joking because within a few days he had found another sleeping arrangement.

After he left, the dogs started to grow tired of whatever was in the house. Early one morning, my daughter's Red Heeler was going absolutely crazy at something in her closet. I heard her yell, "DADDY!" I ran into her room, opened the door, and saw Beau, her Red Heeler, lying on top of her and attacking something that he thought had been in her closet. He would not leave my daughter's bed and was going to shred whatever it was. We brought her, Beau, and Violet to bed with us. Of course, I couldn't find the reason Beau had been so mad, but this was beginning to happen with much more frequency. Because dogs are more perceptive to things than humans, the dogs were sensing something and would go into full attack mode. Just a day later, Violet had something in the hall outside of my daughter's room and was so worked-up she was slobbering. I'm not sure where the noise she was making came from, and I can't even call it barking; it was more like screaming.

A few nights later, my son loaned his room to a houseguest and slept in my daughter's room because she now refused to sleep in there. By two a.m. the lamp had turned itself on twice and the TV turned on once. After the toy Pillsbury Doughboy on her bookcase started giggling, my son exited the room and refused to sleep in there ever again. After both my son and daughter refused to sleep in that room, it became storage.

The remodel was nearing at the halfway point. With my panic attacks and my son nearly severing his arm off during the project, as well as my zombie-like state after almost two years of intermittent sleep, I humorously began to think that something was wrong with the house. I started to put two and two together regarding the previous owners and why they were in such a hurry to evacuate the premises. We used to joke about them laughing at us from their new home while we had to put up with their ghost. A number of my tools and fasteners were being misplaced, and my daughter continued to lose books and toys. And some of these have never been found.

My doctor became a family friend and started having us over to her house on a regular basis. She was trying to get us out of the house so we could calm down and have a break from everything that was going on. The more we told her about our experiences in the house, the more she came to realize that she was correct in assuming that we had some sort of an entity in our house. Not only that, but she truly thought it was an evil one as well. She also believed it was the reason for all of my health issues because she had run a barrage of tests, and they had all come back normal and showed no signs of anything.

Things at work started to get more stressful, and I had to travel farther and farther away from home just to be able to make a living. I thanked God everyday that I had a semi truck as well so that I could do extra to help to keep money coming in. Ironically, when I was in the truck during the week I noticed that my blood pressure issues disappeared and I was able to sleep easily in a rest area in Nebraska or Texas, but when I got home I wasn't able to sleep at all. I think being able to travel and spend time away from the house is what kept me going because I was getting more rest. However, my poor family at home wasn't so lucky. The house was becoming much more active.

At night my son started to hear a little girl's voice outside of his closed bedroom door. He assumed it was my daughter, but when he searched the house for the source of the voice, he found that everyone was asleep. He never did find the source for that little girl's voice.

I had some time while I was on the road, so I decided to draw a map of the backyard so I could start my dream garden the minute I could till the ground in the spring. The garden had three very large plots with a single row for peppers across the front of the main garden bed, which was sort of a centerpiece that was visible from the new family room that I was about to finish remodeling.

I started tilling about two weeks after I drew up the map, and to my surprise I found old, teal-colored fiberglass borders that you could buy in rolls in the 1960s and '70s. I found it very strange that, as I tilled out the beds as I had drawn in my truck a couple weeks ago, I was following exactly how the former beds were placed. There had been no sign of these beds before my groundbreaking, and the yard had been sodded over so long ago that I had to remove a very mature apricot tree from one of the beds before I started tilling. While I was organizing my future garden, my neighbor came to see what I was up to and said the original owner had huge gardens that oddly looked a lot like how mine were shaping up.

Not knowing what else to do about the houses, we eventually took advice from a minister at church. I wanted him to do a walk-through of the house, but was a bit embarrassed because it was still a full-blown construction zone. The minister said it wasn't a problem and suggested that we write scripture verses inside the new walls that we were installing to bring goodness and protection into the house. So, on the back of the drywall I was cutting, my wife promptly wrote several Bible verses in permanent ink before I hung them. Unfortunately, it seemed that this might have actually had the opposite effect than what we were hoping for. Things became noticeably worse in the house within only two days.

I was hauling a load of milk to Illinois when I got a call from home. My daughter was home by herself because she had the day off from school and was literally running out of the house. Doors were slamming and the dogs were going nuts. She put the dogs into the backyard and immediately heard loud footsteps rapidly coming toward her from the dining room into the kitchen. She grabbed her phone and fled from the house. Our neighbor wasn't home, so she called my son's girlfriend, who came and picked her up. My wife was the one who called me, and understandably, she was quite upset. This was the first time we talked about what we should do and questioned if we could put up with any more.

I returned home the following week and was cleaning up after some long days on the road. The bathroom door was cracked a bit to let the steam from the shower out and I heard a girl's voice from outside the door. I couldn't understand what she was saying, but it sounded like my daughter asking me a question.

"What was that, baby?" I asked. But nobody was there. I looked through the whole house and found my whole family was outside, standing by the back fence talking to our neighbor. I shook my head and went back to the bathroom to finish up, but I was interrupted because nature called.

My wife had outfitted the whole house with candles that had LED lights in them that we used for night-lights, because my entire family had become afraid of the dark. The one that sat on the toilet tank would sometimes be stuck after my wife cleaned and would need to be pried off when she would do her weekly cleaning. As I was taking care of my business, I heard the familiar sound of the candle being taken off the lid. I was confronted with a choice—I could either drop everything midstream and catch the candle, or finish what I'm doing and watch the candle slowly slide off the lid and fall onto the floor. I finally just started to laugh. I thought to myself *Who would believe this shit?* I couldn't even start to explain what was going on.

My wife and I went to bed the night of the candle incident. By this time, my wife and I had started to sleep on a hide-a-bed in the mostly furnished office because other parts of the house were still under construction. We had two desktop computers for our businesses and two laptops for the kids for school sitting on an L-shaped desk, so all four screens were visible from the bed. After all of our past issues with the computers turning on in the middle of the night, my wife took extra care to make sure that all four computers were shut down so she would be sure that I could try to have uninterrupted sleep while I was home. She was always worried that I would fall asleep at the wheel on a remote country road somewhere.

I woke up early the next morning and watched the first laptop log on to Windows, soon followed by the second. I woke my wife up, who bolted to an upright position, and we both watched as the business computers turned themselves on and logged on as well. I decided to turn on a movie because I knew I wasn't going to be falling back asleep. I went to the kitchen for something to drink and noticed that the time was two a.m.—the usual time that the computers always seemed to turn on by themselves.

I still wasn't feeling well physically, even though my checkups were fine. I felt like I was ninety years old. I was fatigued, sore, short of breath, and panicky. When I would leave in the semi, I would start to recover and feel better, but I was always worried about my family and what they were dealing with while I was gone. On top of that, money was becoming a major problem.

The day the president officially announced that the 2008 recession was over was exactly the day that our business phones stopped ringing. We couldn't find enough work, and the work we did have before was going to our competitors.

My mood started to change. I was feeling very hurt and angry, and unfortunately it came out in horrible bursts of rage.

I caught an employee of a company we contracted taking kickbacks from other drivers to haul the loads we were contracted to haul. He had a gun and I had steel pipe in my hand, but I wasn't afraid of him. I went completely black with rage. A witness to the event mentioned that he thought I looked like I was possessed. Not knowing what it would mean, the statement he innocently made scared me to death. This behavior had never happened before, and I was very unsettled by how I felt during the incident. I had felt unusually strong; I had no shortness of breath and had no concerns about how big my contender was or if he was armed or not. I was truly not myself. I told my wife what happened and became sick over it. Even though I still think I gave that man what he deserved, I can't explain why I went into such an uncharacteristic rage. I recall very little of what happened, but do know he took my advice to get out of Colorado and never let me see him again. After this incident, I began to withdraw and let my wife handle the business because I just wasn't sure of myself anymore.

Things just kept getting worse at home, too. I had to take my service truck to northern Colorado to get work done. While I was there I would get weekly reports from home, which included doors opening and closing in front of my son and five of his friends. It was around Halloween, so we tried to have a little fun and keep a sense of humor no matter how bad things were getting. Some of our decorations had motion sensors. We had to remove the batteries because just switching them off wasn't enough; you guessed it, they would all go off or turn on in succession at about two o'clock in the morning.

I spent the following Thanksgiving and Christmas in the cab of my welding truck just wishing we could survive, and anxious for the holidays to be over. It was pure misery for me, and my thoughts were becoming even darker. I was ashamed of myself for what my family was going through in the house that I had found and bought for us.

In February of 2011, I left for the North Dakota oilfields. My wife came with and spent the first month with me while my mother stayed at home with the kids. We received three photos from my son in March from the evening of his prom. All the photos were taken from the same cell phone in the dining room at our house. One photo was perfect, but the other two had perfectly visible entities that looked like they were made out of heavy cigarette smoke. One entity was kneeling next to my son's girlfriend, staring at her thighs, and the other one had its head resting on my son's shoulder as if it was posing for the picture with them. The one kneeling looked bald with a deformed face, and the one leaning on my son looked exactly like the devil with a pointed beard and pointed ears. My son showed the picture to my doctor and she immediately said we all had to get out of that house.

It looked like whatever was in the house was mocking and had no intentions of leaving or giving up. This was the last straw for us. I moved my family to a house in Bailey, Colorado, within a month, and we don't know if there are still problems at that house or not.

After realizing there were more things living in that house than us, we decided to look into its history. It looks like we were only the third owners, but just before we were getting ready to move, our neighbor eventually admitted that the original owner was an awful man. He said the man was hitting on the neighbor's teenage daughters when he was almost seventy! It got to the point that my neighbor wouldn't allow his daughters to be in the yard alone. I questioned whether this man might have had an adopted daughter, but my neighbor had no recollection of this. Other than the old man, we couldn't come up with who the other entities on the property may have been.

Make Way for Progress

It was an old house just like any other in Johnston, Iowa, that was once an orchard and farm. It was the first of its kind in the area, but in the last twenty years more houses surrounded it. The west side of the property became prime commercial land where a bank was built, with the noise of cars coming and going replacing the sound of birds, cattle, and chickens. To the east there was valuable residential land. In the early 1970s, houses were built with sprawling lawns and gardens that had children and dogs playing and growing with a nice Iowa upbringing.

In the last ten years, the two-story farmhouse became a neglected mess and the property around it became a place to store junk, dirt piles, and rocks. The potential to make this a beautiful family home was lost forever because the windows were beyond repair, and eventually removed to allow weather into the house, which destroyed it for good. Whoever owned it was probably just considering the value of the lot, and assumed the home was worth nothing.

In the fall of the year, the house was used as a training facility for the local fire department. They practiced various techniques and burned the old farmhouse to the ground little by little. Of course, they skillfully controlled the burn, which enabled the bulk of the burning structure to fall into the foundation where it would continue to smolder for a couple of days.

The morning of one of the burns, Jennifer was on her way to work at a restaurant in the neighboring town when she noticed there was a traffic control officer and saw the firefighters working the scene. She didn't give it much thought, but knew that eventually something would need to be done with the abandoned house. Thanks to an exceptionally busy night at work, she had forgotten all about the farmhouse.

It was during her drive home later that night that things got a little out of sorts for her. Getting off of work at eleven p.m., Jennifer just wanted to get home and hoped that her family was still up so they could watch a movie or do something fun. She hated coming home to a sleeping family because, with her crazy hours, she felt like she missed all the fun. As she got within a mile of the old house, she suddenly began to have a feeling of overwhelming sadness. She said she started to cry, but couldn't figure out why.

As she turned onto the road that passed the old house, she noticed it was just a pile of ash and coals, with smoke coming from the smoldering house that was drifting across the street. As she passed the house, she was wiping tears from her cheeks. She looked in the rearview mirror to wipe off her running mascara when she noticed a figure standing in the middle of the road behind her, so she stopped. Jennifer wiped her eyes and looked in the mirror again. Noticing that the figure was still there, she physically turned to look through the back window to see who it could be. The figure seemed more transparent than a real person and was more of a dark shadow standing in the smoke, but Jennifer couldn't make out any other details. She immediately stepped on the gas and sped home, unsure of why she was feeling the way she was or what exactly it was she saw behind her in the street. All we know is that something or someone is linked to that old farmhouse and when it burned they were sad about it, and Jennifer attached to that.

Rock and Roll

We have all been witness to people who chase their dreams and those who don't. Those who did have always amazed me with the places their journeys have taken them. The end result may have been far from the intended goal, but no matter what, they are doers. They are people who gave it their best shot and can look back at what they did and know they did their best. My friend, Ed Gillman, was one of those people.

Growing up in the 1980s, with a remarkable love and drive for rock music, it seemed only natural for him and some friends to form a band and give it a go, which he did! First of all, he had the hair for it. It was the age of the hair bands, and with the hair and the attitudes, it seemed like everything else just fell into place for him. I know it wasn't just that easy because, from time to time, I would hear about the trials they had to get the magical combination of sound and commitment that was required. They were doing this at a time when there was mounting responsibilities in life, and were surrounded by girls, and groupies, and constant competition from other bands. All of this brought them barrel loads of drama that constantly obstructed their dream of becoming the "next big thing."

Years later, we met up and I was given the thrill of looking at some of his photos from the 1980s and '90s, and was in complete amazement at where his music had taken him and the band. First, I saw pictures of him with some very well-known musicians backstage somewhere. Then there were pictures of the band in action onstage, but my most favorite picture was taken when they were in their prime, under a bridge in Norwoodville, Iowa, and they were in their glory. That picture captured a generation in microcosm for me. It was the '80s at their absolute best. The long hair, the boots, the shredded jeans, the leather coats, and the in-your-face attitude that made them what they were—rockers. But rockers aren't immune to the paranormal. In fact, it seemed like they even attracted a certain degree of the unexplained or unwanted experiences.

One occurrence that they remember vividly is when they allowed someone who lives wickedly to hang around the band during their early years. He seemed harmless enough at first, and seemed to just like to hang out with the band

and listen to rehearsals. One day, one of the band members jokingly mentioned that this guy drove a car without any mirrors. It was obvious this young man didn't like to look at himself, whether it was because of guilt, shame, or some weird phobia. The band members soon noticed the man was pretty deep into the drug scene and had full intentions of luring the lead guitar player from the band, which he eventually did. Despite all of this, it was his manner that was the strangest of all. He was very dark, and if there was ever any mention of God or Jesus he went crazy and started cursing and mumbling to himself, revealing that he had no respect for either the Father or the Son.

After he was done with his destruction of the band and moved on, the remaining members started to realize how truly evil this guy had been. They started to talk about some of the weird things he would do and say. It was a relief that he was gone, but coincidently, every time the band talked about him, something went wrong. At first, it was small things like technical glitches with the electronic equipment, but as time went on, things started to go a little worse. One night while practicing in Ed's garage, the subject of the young man came up and they talked about the usual recollections. The drummer's girlfriend asked them to stop because she was so afraid of something bad happening. Right at that moment, a breaker blew out and the whole garage went black. They all screamed and left the garage. It took Ed a few minutes to get the power back on, but when everyone went back, they noticed that the crucifix above the practice room was hanging upside down. That pretty much ended practice for that night, and they agreed to never speak of that young man again. To this day, Ed feels nothing but apprehension about this subject, and is even uneasy with this much information being out.

Ed later moved to a house in east Des Moines, and along with the new house there was a new band. Ed's house became a regular meeting place for the band with many late-night jam sessions. At the end of one of those sessions, in the early morning hours, the lead singer was struck and killed by a car in front of the house. It was a devastating blow to everybody, and it seems like it is an emotional wound that just doesn't want to heal. The unfortunate accident is not the strangest part. A few months later, some bizarre things started to happen at the house.

The first of several occurrences happened one evening when Ed returned home from work. His friend, Jeff, and his brother were in the basement playing guitars. Ed let them know he was home and proceeded to the couch to watch the news. The telephone rang, so Ed put the TV remote next to him on the floor and answered the phone. After hanging up the phone a few minutes later, Ed reached for the remote, but it wasn't where he had placed it. He searched under the couch, in the cushions, and then the whole living room, but came up with nothing. Nobody had come from downstairs, nor did Ed even leave the couch during the phone call. Ed went to the basement to tell Jeff and his brother what had happened. While he was explaining what had happened, Ed glanced at a box sitting next to the furnace. On top of that box was the remote.

Almost the same thing happened with a postage stamp that was put on the kitchen table that was going to be used to mail a bill. After using the bathroom, Ed went back to the table to write out the check and envelope to mail it the next morning, and the stamp was gone. He spent several minutes searching not only the entire kitchen, but the whole house as well. Coming up with nothing, Ed became furious, so he went to take a shower. Afterward, he returned to the kitchen and there was the stamp right in the middle of the table. Ed was alone with the doors and windows locked.

The trouble doesn't end here for my friend Ed. After a particularly hard day at work, he decided that maybe a bath would be the ticket to unwind instead of his usual evening shower. Just as he picked up the shampoo bottle, something pounded several times on the bathroom door, less than four feet from the tub. Terrified, Ed dropped the shampoo bottle and stared at the door, unsure of what to do. After a couple of long minutes, he gathered the courage to get up and open the door to see what was there. Once again, there was nothing there. Again, nobody else was in the house and the doors were locked.

Things only seemed to accelerate as time went on, and they became a little more disturbing. Frequently, Ed would hear what sounded like keys being laid down, and the living room light would turn on in the middle of the night. He would always leave the bedroom door partially open and could see the light come on in the living room. Then it would move to the hallway light. As soon as he would jump out of bed, the lights would shut off simultaneously. As usual, he was all alone at home and the doors were locked.

During this time Ed was visited by his friend Doug, who had just returned from a trip to Texas. Ed had a cable rock music channel on TV, and the remote was sitting next to him on the arm of his chair. While Ed and Doug were talking about Texas, Doug noticed that the song "Deep in the Heart of Texas" was now playing on the TV. Somehow, the channel had been changed to country, but the volume was down low enough that they didn't notice it right away.

Soon after that, Ed and his girlfriend were watching TV on a Saturday night. Ed always had a VCR on and ready in case something came on that he liked and wanted to tape. All the lights were off, Ed's girlfriend was asleep on the couch, and he was asleep on the floor next to the couch. Ed was awakened by his girlfriend who was talking in her sleep, and it sounded as if she were talking backward. Kind of frightened, Ed turned to the VCR to see what time it was and noticed that the tape counter was turning backward. Only the counter was going backward, not the tape itself. Not only that, but Ed noticed the VCR was turned off completely. He quickly woke up his girlfriend and she was able to see the tape counter stop. This never happened again.

The last problem arose one night when Ed's friend Jeff was spending the night in the guest room. Jeff burst into the room, terrified that he had seen a large black figure hovering over his bed. Ed questioned him at first, but had to believe him after all that had happened in the house recently. Soon after, Ed's girlfriend bought him a Cocker Spaniel puppy. Almost immediately the little dog sensed something in the house. It barked repeatedly at the hallway or at one specific corner of the living room that faced the street. Sometimes it would bark for hours just at those specific spots. This constant barking went on for about three or four weeks, and then suddenly it just stopped. We will never know whether the little dog possessed enough power to scare off whatever was causing trouble in the house or whether the entity just decided it was time to move on. Either way, the trouble stopped for Ed after that.

Eternal Guilt

The forlorn little bungalow is still standing in the lonely town of Russell Gulch, Colorado, west of Denver. The house and town are slowly turning to dust 150 years after its heyday as a mining town in one of the richest gold and silver mining areas in the state. If there were ever a house or location that is overburdened with residual energy, it is this place. Some areas are prone to attract wickedness, and the little bungalow in Russell Gulch is no different.

A particularly nasty man named Azel lived in this house and worked as the manager and bookkeeper of the Topeka Mine in 1901, which was a very lofty position to hold at the turn of the century. He was in charge of business and finances, so when the mine fell into financial trouble, Azel was retained by the owner to finalize the mine's affairs, which included the burden of regular trips to Denver. These trips kept him away from home for weeks at a time.

Azel was married to Jennie, the daughter of a minister, and had one son Donald, born in 1895. However, while in Denver, Azel met a woman by the name of Lottie and the relationship quickly turned to an affair. There was not a real commitment between the two; it was more of a purely physical relationship. Azel later admitted that he had never told Lottie he was married and she had never asked him to marry her.

His time in Denver with Lottie turned to sin, alcohol, gambling, and debt. He started embezzling from his employer to sustain his habits and was eventually caught and relieved of his duties for the Topeka Mine, which he told no one. His loving wife and son knew nothing of his frivolities. All they understood was that Azel was not home much.

In winter of 1904 Azel returned home from one of his trips, but the burdens of his affair and his criminal activity overtook him. He was in love with Lottie, was having trouble at work, and was sure that his secret life would soon be revealed to his wife and son. He was running out of time. On February 20, 1904, Azel was in bed with his wife, Jennie, and was hiding his revolver under his pillow. While talking to her, he pulled the .32-caliber out from under his pillow and shot his unsuspecting wife in the head. The bullet went all the way through and she died instantly. Azel recovered the bullet from the bedding, removed her wedding ring, and put both the bullet and ring in his pocket and covered Jennie up with the bedding. He later pawned the wedding ring for cash.

He then called his nine-year-old son, Donald, who was outside playing at the time, into the house. He told Donald that his mother was sleeping and to look at a bird that was outside the window. While Donald looked away, Azel shot him in the back of the head. He laid his son's body on the bed, put the bullet it in his pocket, and covered the dead nine-year-old with a blanket next to his mother.

According to the murder testimony, after the shootings Azel got drunk on whatever alcohol was in the house and hitched a ride back to Denver. He returned to the house several times to take things of value to pay debts, and on one trip even killed the family dog and disposed of him behind the shed. People in town assumed the family was traveling together, but the owner of the house knew the family was months behind on the rent so decided to stop by the house and see if they had slipped away. The landlord's wife went over to the house, saw Donald's body on the bed, and fled to report what she had found. Within hours, both bodies were found forty-seven days after they were killed.

The sheriff from Gilpin County, wondering why Azel was gone, went to Denver where he was in jail for writing a bad check. The sheriff questioned him about his family's murder and he admitted to the crime without any hesitation. The sheriff took Azel into custody and brought him back to Gilpin County. A lynch mob, who demanded that Azel be handed over to them so they could give Jennie and Donald justice properly, immediately confronted him. The sheriff convinced the mob that he wasn't worth the trouble, and they eventually went back to doing whatever lynch mobs do when they are not lynching stuff.

While in jail, Azel wrote several letters to Lottie. To his dismay, none of the letters were answered. Azel could not understand why she would abandon him in such a manner. When Azel went to trial, he immediately confessed his guilt and the jury almost immediately sentenced him to death. Shortly thereafter, Azel was transported back to the prison to await his fate. On March 6, 1905, Azel was hanged.

His last words were for Lottie, "I waited for you."

Jennie and Donald were buried in a single grave at a cemetery in Fort Collins, but there are no reports about what was done with Azel's body after the execution and autopsy. It may have gone to science or an unmarked grave of the lowest form near the location of his execution.

The house today is a tormented, dark place and is rumored to be very haunted. The locals in Russell Gulch call it "the murder house." It is rundown and in very sad shape, surrounded by distorted trees and scattered ruins of the past. A paranormal research group by the name of Spirit Realm Investigative Project (SRIP) performed an investigation on the property in an attempt to ease the activity at the location. Learning the history of the property and the reported activity, the lead investigator of the group, LeeAnna, fully expected to find evidence that it was indeed Jennie and Donald still in the residence. Reports indicated a horrible feeling of grief and despair associated with the alleged haunting, but what LeeAnna encountered was a bit of a surprise. Upon entering the property, a member of her team began communicating with an entity, that clearly stated that it wasn't a mother and child—but it was the killer. The spirit was indeed Azel. At first, LeeAnna wanted nothing to do with this spirit considering who he was and what he did. Through communication, however, the team learned that it would be impossible for him to pass on, so the goal to cleanse the property could not be met.

LeeAnna explained to me that he was remorseful and considered this his punishment for the murders and infidelity. The haunting of the property continues to this day, and there is even interaction with this same entity in the area of the old Gilpin County jail, where Azel was detained until he was sent to the prison in Canon City for execution. People who have had contact with this being indicate feelings of depression and pain mixed with great sorrow.

What do you do with a guilty ghost that won't leave? I guess you live with it or move on. I for one truly believe that being stuck for eternity is the appropriate punishment for this kind of crime. Although for privacy purposes I cannot reveal the exact location of the house, it is relatively easy to find if you do some research or talk to the locals. I highly recommend that you take a drive up there on a blustery day and stop in town for a few minutes, and then examine the feelings that come over you in that short period of time. Is it anxiety, fear, or a feeling that you just want to move on and eat your picnic lunch somewhere else?

A Summer in the Past

Virginia is inherently old and full of history and was at one time home to very affluent families, one of which I call my own. Being Virginians since 1617, my family was at the forefront of major historical events. Of course, I had no choice but to become a history and a Civil War buff thanks to our frequent visits back to the homestead, sitting on my grandmother's lap as she told me stories of my great-grandfather and his experiences as a Confederate artilleryman. My favorite stories were of Robert E. Lee and the cunning John Singleton Moseby.

With most stories from Virginia there always seem to be a presence to accompany them. There is always at least one spirit to verify or keep alive some major event in history. One of my aunt's homes in Orange County, Virginia, was such a place. It was burdened with grief and spectral visitors. Although in a heavily wooded area, trench fortifications were easily found on the acreage, as well as mounds that were believed to be burial sites. Many artifacts from the Civil War were found on the property, right down to ammunition and sidearms. I loved it because it was in the woods and was a great place to play. Just after dark, however, it became a little different. Sitting on the covered patio, I would hear another year's worth of stories that my aunt and grandmother would tell about living here.

About a mile down the road sat a large farmhouse that had survived the Civil War. One night while I was asleep in the back seat of our big station wagon, I was awakened to hear my mom ask Dad, "Did you see that?"

Dad jokingly replied, "Nope, didn't see a damned thing." They had both seen a white, wispy vapor walk right across the tree-covered lane, heading to the old square farmhouse. About an hour later, my cousin and his family pulled into the driveway. My cousin was laughing, but his wife was frantic.

She threw the car door open and yelled to us on the patio from the dark driveway, "You will never guess what we saw." It was at exactly the same place of our sighting less than an hour before.

Grandma would talk of hearing voices out in the trees behind the house. They sounded distant and would always say "Hey. Is that you?" as if they were looking for someone. The voice had an eerie kind of echo in the dense forest that surrounded the acreage, and was hard to determine which direction it was coming from.

Doors would open and close in the house, and sometimes Grandma would even have a visitor. Shortly before my grandmother discovered she had cancer, which she successfully beat, she was awoken to two stern-faced people standing at the foot of her bed. They were just standing there staring at her. They were dressed in clothing from the Colonial Period. She assumed it was a man and wife; the man was wearing a tricorn hat and the woman was wearing a white bonnet. After a few long minutes, they just faded away. Shortly after her battle with cancer they visited again in the same manner, but this time they had a pleasant look on their faces and then faded off.

Grandma was no stranger to unwanted visitors. Many times she and my aunts would chase a man wearing a top hat and cape from their home in Alexandria, Virginia, during the 1920s and '30s. He was dressed in the fashions of the mid-1800s. His last visit was in 1943 while my father was on a short leave from the Navy before being sent to the Pacific Theater. He was asleep on the couch when he heard one of his sisters start to scream, which in turn started all the women screaming. Dad jumped from the couch in his underwear and began his pursuit of the caped invader out into the alley behind the house. The invader vanished into the night and has never been seen again. For several years my dad searched for any good explanation as to who it could be. To my aunts and grandmother it was a ghost, but even though Dad was very skeptical of hauntings, he could never seem to rule that out. It is funny, though, that during the rest of my father's life, he absolutely refused to buy anything other than a brand-new house. I guess he had his superstitions.

Lastly is the old family home near Troy, Virginia. There is a new house that stands within the foundation of the old house, which was built in the years following the Civil War. In the tall grass out back is our family cemetery, which includes a few unmarked graves. The home has long since been out of the family, but the people who bought it in the 1970s would allow us to visit and kept in touch with my aunt, letting her know they were welcome to visit anytime. It's your family, they would say.

Shortly after they moved into the house, the new owners began to inquire about a certain family member, and even gave an accurate description of him. He had been seen out by the barn next to where they chop wood. One day they were splitting wood and turned to see him a few yards away, just smiling and watching them work. He also visited them in the barn. He was standing in the door with his arms crossed and seemed pleased with whatever was going on. Their description matched that of one of my ancestors, my great-grandfather's brother, who had lived there during the 1800s. The reason for his visits have never been known, and the owners were not afraid, but loved their ghost and tried to make him feel welcome.

Maybe it's the way we lived. Maybe it is because of a better connection with past relatives. Some families are just more sensitive than others to the paranormal. In the case of my family, the connections are still there and the channels are still open, constantly tugging at my heart and soul, pulling me home if even for just a short while. I love the Rocky Mountains, but my heart belongs to Fluvanna County, Virginia.

chapter two

Vocational Ghosts and Other Disruptions

What on earth is a vocational ghost? It's basically an apparition that visits you at work. I find these stories to be the most credible because the storyteller is at work, and if they are doing what they were suppose to be doing, ghosts should have been the last thing on their mind. Picture a dark, stormy night working in a rail yard, piloting a tractor-trailer through a dangerous thunderstorm two hours behind schedule, or being a state trooper at the scene of an accident on a lonely country road. The minds of these individuals should be concerned with the situation at hand. There should be no time for imaginations to run wild. Somehow though, things still happen in these situations that make people wonder if their minds are wandering or if they saw what they really think they did. The stories in this chapter involve people just trying to get to quitting time. It is most definitely dedicated to the hardworking men and women.

More Than a Second Chance

A very good friend of mine, Adam, who I have known for more than thirty years had a life-changing experience, years before he should have had to figure out what life really is. At the age of eight while on vacation with his family in South Dakota, he was reaching over the edge for a ball that was floating in their motel swimming pool. His family was close by, but they were engrossed in a conversation. The ball was just out of reach and every time he could touch it, the ball would float out a bit farther away. He tried to reach a bit too far and fell into the pool.

He didn't know how to swim, but remembers fighting the water and eventually beginning to tire and slow down after a few seconds. At that point, he remembers floating to the bottom. He clearly remembers then what he believed to be a female voice telling him to fight. He started to kick and paddle, but still continued to sink to the bottom. He recalls a feeling of calmness come over him, as he seemed to enter a tunnel that was at first dark before turning light. He didn't have any thoughts of his family or what was happening, but he remembers it as a good feeling, like it was right. At about that same time, my friend's father recalls having a horrible feeling come over him and a voice prompting him to check on his son. His father jumped up and saw his son's body at the bottom of the pool. Both my friend's parents jumped into the water, grabbed him, and pulled him to the surface. Adam could hear his parents frantically trying to get him out of the water. His mother didn't have enough strength to pull him from the water and had to let him go, but he fell onto his father's shoulders, which caused him to spit up some water, but he still wasn't breathing. Adam could hear everything, but had the sensation that he was still in the tunnel.

Adam's life was obviously saved that day, but along with his second chance, he believes another ability was born into his consciousness. He seemed to have developed a sort of unwanted psychic ability. Throughout his childhood, he started to realize that he could see what people were thinking, and more importantly, whether someone was a good person with good intentions, or the opposite.

By the time he turned eighteen, what Adam considered a burden kind of ran wild with him. He described it like listening to a radio that was receiving one hundred radio stations all at once. It was overpowering and happening on a daily basis. He begged God to make it stop because it was becoming too much for him to handle. He could even sense if a negative spirit or entity was present.

I can remember him having a lot of headaches in those days, but I never thought it was related to something so incredible. Adam's prayers were partly answered. Although he never lost his ability, he was able to gain control of it, but not completely.

This became very evident during an incident while he was working as a maintenance man at a church in Des Moines, Iowa. Adam said the church was overwhelming for him because there was too much going on in the building. Through this job he learned that some churches serve God, and He was there, while others were on another path—an evil path without God. The church my friend worked at was one of the latter. One day he was cleaning the sanctuary when he sensed an evil presence above him in the balcony messing with him. Adam tried to ignore it, but the black, human-shaped entity was infuriating him to the point that he couldn't take any more. He looked up to the balcony and decided to go up there to see exactly what it was that was bothering him. He started the climb to the balcony, but found he could not get past the fourth step. It was as if something as holding him back and trying to tell him he shouldn't go up to the balcony.

He went back to the sanctuary, looked up at the balcony, and out loud said, "I have this ability. Basically, you are nothing, and if you want to, let's go." Boy, was that the wrong thing to say.

Immediately, this human-sized entity grew until it was enormous, and it became extremely aggressive, obviously angered that somebody would challenge it. It scared Adam pretty bad because he had gotten himself into something he couldn't handle. He started apologizing for what he said, but that didn't work. It was too late. The entity let Adam know it could kill him instantly. Adam said it was communicating with him telepathically. He could even tell how it was going to kill him. It was going to make him have a heart attack.

Without turning around, Adam sensed another larger presence behind him who spoke to the evil entity and said, "He doesn't know what he is doing."

The entity replied that he was going to kill Adam, and what Adam could only identify as an angel said, "No, you are not." Adam got the feeling of being disciplined and realized how foolish he was for openly challenging an evil entity. The presence sort of faded away, and shortly thereafter the angel faded away as well.

Soon after this happened, Adam was cleaning up after a wedding and was running a vacuum. He started to see what appeared to be a dance in progress in the room. It looked to be a very large ball. The people at this ball were wearing clothes that were worn in the 1930s.

A man looked over at him and said, "You are bothering us."

"Excuse me?" Adam said.

"The vacuum," the man said. "Can't you see we are trying to have a dance here?"

They came to an agreement that Adam would do a quick job and get out of their way. Oddly enough, they all seemed satisfied with this idea. This church is only one of the many properties in Des Moines that have reported spirits, but the story of a ball has never been discovered.

Believe it or not, Adam's biggest problem is antique shops. He said that they are very hard for him to handle. It is as if each piece in those places is carrying some sort of energy, and he receives it all at once. Within a few minutes, it becomes very overwhelming for him. Events like these occur for Adam on a daily basis, with everything and everyone he comes in contact with. Adam in no way considers this a gift; he gets no pleasure from it, and after so many years, has just accepted it.

Railroaders

Most strange stories come from engineers and conductors, riding the rails at all hours of the night dealing with the bad weather, schedules, and hundreds of other afflictions that come with the industry. However, the carmen are a relatively unknown group of railroaders that have more stories to tell than any other trade on the rails. They inspect the train, respond to derailments, and repair cars either in the yard or at very remote locations that occur because of hotboxes or wheel failures. They walk the trains in dark yards late at night armed with just a portable two-way radio, a lantern, and a buggy bar, inspecting for defects before they are cut up and assembled into another train. The carmen deal with bad weather, absolute darkness, vagrants, thieves, and occasional happenings that have no explanation. Of course, the night shift always seems to see the most action.

Many years ago in a rail yard in Des Moines, a horrific event took place that made some carmen quit their jobs completely and find work in other industries. All it took was one bad decision in a moment of carelessness for a night shift carman to be coupled into a train. He was attempting to cross the track on foot in front of a cut of cars. It was a cold and rainy night, and train cars are almost completely silent on wet rails. He obviously didn't look up to see the cars that were being kicked into the track he was trying to cross because as he crossed in front of the cut, the moving cars coupled into his lower abdomen and crushed him into the couplers. He was still alive when another carman found him after noticing that he was missing. The first responders knew that the couplers themselves were actually keeping him alive and as soon as the cars were pulled apart the man would die.

At the adamant request of the other carmen, his wife was picked up at their house and brought to the rail yard to say goodbye. The injured carman held hands with his wife and his best friend as the train was slowly pulled apart.

"He just fell asleep and we all cried," his best friend recalled as the train was pulled apart. These tough railroaders surrounded their fallen comrade and cried. However, even though he was no longer alive, the departed carman seems to have lingered on to protect his friends. In the same area of the yard where the accident happened, there have been a number of strange occurrences.

A few months after the accident, a night shift carman was on foot crossing the track in front of a cut of cars when he felt someone grab his collar, pull him back, and throw him onto the ground. The only problem is that there was no one there.

Several months after that, a unit train heading to Kansas City was preparing to enter the yard from the east and was slowing for the east yard switch. The engineer used the radio to identify the train, and the yardmaster replied that a carman was at the east switch and had him lined up for track six. The engineer was set to bring her into the yard, cut the power, and take them to the MIC for service. The engineer replied his understanding, throttled the train, and eased it into the yard. About halfway into the yard, the engineer noticed a blue lantern in the middle of the track where there is a slight curve. He set the air, throttled down to a stop, and notified the yardmaster on the radio that he had a blue light on track six and couldn't proceed. The rear of his train was holding up the east yard for the switch crew and shut everything down. A carman on the west side of the yard drove over to see what was going on, but knew that he and the other carmen were just there aligning the switches for this train.

Sure enough, when he got to the track there was a glowing blue lantern. The blue lantern is a signal that only carmen use and all other railroad employees must yield to. It was placed right next to a broken rail that would have put the locomotives on the ground. It was at the location where the accident had happened, and the rail men knew it was their fallen brother giving them a warning.

The unexplained events started to fade over time. The responsibility of reliving the stories fell into the hands of the retired carmen remembering the days of their youth with the storms, floods, hobos, and their fallen friend who decided he just wasn't done playing with trains and decided to keep an eye out for his brothers. Maybe the stories will help to keep an overambitious carman just starting his career to take that extra minute to just be safe.

The West Yard

Rail yards are extremely dangerous places. It doesn't matter if you are a ghost hunter or a train buff, you are taking your life into your own hands by trespassing on railroad property.

The men and women who work in such locations are trained to assess the risks and protect themselves from the dangers associated with their jobs. Because of this, the location of the yard in the following story must be kept secret, but it is an operational yard in the western United States.

It seemed to be an unusually long night for the crew of carmen working the night shift. The slowing of the economy in 2008 created a big slowdown on train schedules, which made the night shift very long and boring. On a cold February morning, things were about to change drastically for an entire crew and their supervisor. A westbound train hauling coal was being assembled in the west yard. No one really liked working in the west yard. So much so that the yard operations manager usually refrained from assembling trains in that part of the yard. It was out of sight from the tower, difficult for carmen and crew to access, and was dark. He just didn't feel it was safe for the night shift.

On this night the train originated on a branch that entered into the west yard on a wye track from the south, so it would have been inconvenient to move the train to the east yard to add cars, inspect it, and add multiple power units. This train was long and heavy, and required the use of remote engines on the rear of the train, which would assist the unit train over mountainous terrain. At two o'clock in the morning the yard manager radioed two carmen to go to the west yard and lace the train as cars were added to the rear of train. By the time that job is finished, the train crew should be onboard to link the remote locomotives and assist with the mandatory air brake tests.

The two carmen headed to the train to begin their task. One was on foot walking and lacing the air hoses, and the other carman followed him in a truck with bright floodlights for light to work by, and to do a visual inspection while they progressed down the length of the 105-car train. The worker on foot climbed into the head end of the locomotive and sent air to the train. He would be doing what they call chasing air all the way down to the rear of the train. This is done so if there were an air leak he would hear it, ensuring that all the air hoses and plumbing are laced and airtight.

Two other carmen were sitting in their truck in the east yard waiting for an incoming train, and listening to the radio traffic of the other crew in the west yard because they knew that yard had a reputation of being unsafe. Vagrants and train hoppers were common in that area, and if the men in the west yard needed help they could be there in a hurry. The two men heard the train crew was onboard to help with the air test and linking the remotes.

Over the radio they kept hearing, "Where is it now? Again? I can't explain this." Knowing that the air test shouldn't take more than an hour and hearing the frustration of the train crew over the radio, the two carmen in the east yard asked if the other crew needed help. They quickly replied yes and instructed them to go to the rear of the train by the remotes and turn all of their floodlights on. The west yard crew needed as much light as they could get. This prompted the night supervisor to head that way as well with his truck to provide even more light.

The east yard crew arrived and turned on their lights as they were instructed, and the train conductor stepped off of the locomotive and came to talk to them. Understandably, he was very frustrated because the train was now more than an hour behind schedule. The east yard guys asked him what was wrong.

"Man, I don't know," the conductor replied. "We tested out and were leaving the yard when the air busted. I have walked this damned train three times on three different attempts to test, and right when we are ready to test, we bust air and find hoses disconnected between the cars. I think someone is screwing with us or these boys don't know how to lace a train."

The second carmen from the east crew grabbed a light, a buggy bar, and a portable two-way radio and decided to walk the train and double-check everything. The supervisor followed in on the other side of the train with his truck to back him up, absolutely positive that they were going to catch a vagrant somewhere on the length of the train. While these two were double-checking the train, the conductor and other east crew member stood by the truck with the floodlights on, and focused on the train to be sure they would see if anything was out of the ordinary. In total, there were six people watching the train from all angles. They didn't find any issues or trespassers, so one of the west carmen radioed the engineer and said everything looked good. He instructed the engineer to let them know when he had air and was ready to test. Within twenty minutes the engineer was ready. Both the east and west carmen readied their trucks with the floodlights glowing so they could both drive the length of the train to double the coverage and check for a proper application test.

WHOOOSH. The air busted again. A huge cloud of dust blew up ten cars ahead of the remote engines indicating where the failure occurred. The engineer was very upset and made it perfectly clear over the radio. The supervisor cursed and ran to the area of the leak with the west end carmen right behind him. Once again, the lines were perfectly disconnected. The supervisor stated whoever was screwing with them knew their shit, meaning they understood how the train works. There was complete and total frustration because it would have been impossible for anyone to slip past all of them with all of the lights, moving trucks, and six sets of eyes watching the train like a hawk.

The engineer reset the train out of emergency and radioed that he was ready to send the air back. "AGAIN!" he screamed.

This time the carmen spread out over the train and walked it in quarters while the conductor, supervisor, and engineer kept watch on the train. WHOOOSH. The air indicator barely moved. Another line was disconnected, exhausting all air on the rear of the train. One carman was almost right next to the breach. He was so close that his co-workers heard him shout a few choice words, and was trying to clean the dirt from his eyes. The others ran to him to make sure he was okay because they were all unsure as to why he was cursing. They thought he had caught someone in the act and was actually fighting them, which of course wasn't what was happening. The entire group decided to reorganize their thoughts and strategies, and figure out what the hell was going on.

As they all stood in the beams of the floodlights with buggy bars in hand, they were absolutely sure that someone was tampering with the train. It was then that they all heard a hideous and evil laugh coming from the direction of an abandoned train station on the property. This laugh was loud enough to be heard over the sound of leaking air, three idling trucks, and six idling locomotives.

The supervisor looked at his crew, and with a perplexed look on his face said, "Ummmmm ... okay." After this they re-laced the leaking cars, successfully tested the train, and sent it on its way exactly five hours late.

The crew doesn't care to talk about this night, but they are even less enthusiastic to work in the west yard at night. The events of this night have never been explained, and given the location of the train, there was nowhere to hide without running through the beam of the lights and into plain site of the carmen and train crew. The abandoned station was more that 100 yards away, and the men never saw an actual person other than themselves do anything to tamper with the train. No one knows where that laugh really came from.

It must be understood that tampering with a train is a federal offense. It is punishable under the Patriot Act and can result in jail time.

The Bakken Wells

I spent some time working in the oilfields of North Dakota. The workdays in the oil patch are quite different. The gloves are taken off and we get serious. A minimum of twelve-hour workdays is required, days off are a luxury seldom enjoyed, and there is usually only time for work or sleep. There is no time for goofing around. I knew nothing of North Dakota. Obviously, it must get cold up there, but that was the end of what I knew about the area. That is, until one very cold morning in March 2011.

At around nine a.m., a very upset driver and truck pusher came to the shop three hours late to swap out for the day shift. Earlier that morning, at around two, the driver arrived at one of the locations near Mandaree. This is on an Indian reservation and is almost the epicenter of drilling activity on the Bakken oil formation. He positioned his truck to load production water off of this location to take to a disposal site. The location had at least eight to ten inches of sloppy mud with a frozen base underneath and was surrounded in at least three feet of heavy, wet, melting snow with pretty heavy fog in the surrounding area. This location, as well as many others in the area, had a flare pit with a large flame that lit up the location pretty well. The other flare pits lit up the fog, so the area was pretty well lit up but casting a lot of shadows. The driver exited the cab of his truck after engaging the vacuum pump, which is very noisy, went to the rear of the truck to connect his hose to the location tank, and take a reading. As he was hooking up the hose, he realized that he needed an adapter.

As he walked back toward his tractor, he heard a loud slam and thought the door on the well house had slammed shut. When he walked into the shadows around the front of his truck he stopped and found himself face to face with who he later described as a very tall, dark-skinned, and terrifying looking man. The driver was very startled but managed to ask this man if he could help him. The other man turned and ran off into the snow, disappearing into the dark. The driver immediately got on his two-way radio and reported what was clearly a security breach.

It took the better part of a half hour for a sheriff's deputy and a tribal police officer to arrive after being led to the location by the on-duty truck pusher. The driver told the officers what had happened, and they started to look over the area. Within a few minutes, the tribal officer asked the driver to clarify exactly where he had run into this man and exactly which direction he had run. The driver walked the officer to the very spot, told him about hearing the door slam on the well house, and pointed in the exact direction the man had run.

The tribal officer turned to the driver, the sheriff's deputy, and the pusher and said, "I would like to say a prayer over you to protect you and your family."

The driver just chuckled and said, "Okay. Why?" The sheriff's deputy answered by saying there was only one set of footprints—the driver's.

The driver became defensive and tried to convince the officers that he wasn't lying. To this the tribal officer said, "You are not the first one. What you saw was evil." The driver then allowed the tribal office to say his prayer.

As time went on, the stories kept coming from the fields in Mandaree. Sometimes drivers would laugh about it, as if they were getting used to these kinds of interactions with what they described as skinwalkers, evil spirits, or simply humans that don't leave footprints in the mud or snow. The drivers would act as if this was a common occurrence, and that when going out to these fields, it was more than likely you would see something similar.

A driver from another company told me another story. He was driving to a location in January 2011 on a gravel road plowed only wide enough for one semi to pass through. It was about two miles to his destination, the road was very icy, and the temperature was about thirty-eight degrees below zero. He had one hill to climb and no room for error. If he would lose control and spin out, he could have been there for several hours before help could get to him.

As he crested over the hill, his headlights caught what appeared to be a man without a shirt on walking in the same direction he was headed. He said at first it startled him because it's not common to see hitchhikers that far out, but as he passed, he remembered thinking it was almost forty degrees below zero. This man would die out here. The driver began to slow to a stop as he turned on his lights in the rear of the truck, while looking in his mirrors to see if the guy was going to run up to the truck and get warm. The driver didn't see him, so he set the brakes, got out of his truck, and walked to the rear of the truck.

"Hey! Are you out there? Can I get you some help?" he yelled into the darkness. There was no answer to any of his questions. The driver got on his radio and alerted his dispatcher and the other drivers about the shirtless man, but no one else saw him, there were no stalled cars on the road, and there weren't any houses for several miles. There was never an explanation about the shirtless man.

Another driver was at one of the Bakken well locations and had an incident there as well. He was pulling a load of production water at about eleven p.m. when he went to his tractor to get a pair of warm gloves. His vacuum pump was running, which is so loud that you can't hear anything else around you. The driver jumped into the cab and found a man sitting in his passenger seat, just staring straight out the front window. The driver told me he fell straight back out of the truck and landed flat on his back in the snow. The fall knocked the wind out of him for a few seconds, but he got back up and screamed at the intruder while grabbing a pipe wrench that he kept inside the door. When he got up to confront the intruder, he realized the man was gone, the passenger door was closed, and nothing in his truck seemed out of place.

The driver notified his boss, but they never found any evidence that there had been a man in the passenger seat. No wet footprints from the melting snow in the warm cab, nothing.

Finally is the most-talked-about apparition in the area. It seems that if a driver or a pusher hasn't yet seen what others describe as a naked Native American on a horse at full gallop, running across the frozen hills and gulches of western North Dakota, they soon expect to, and will. This man has only been seen at night and has so far only been near the various well locations on the reservation. Some tribal members I have spoken to call him an omen because the spirits are upset with what is happening to their people.

Some say that Native American legends warned of the black blood coming from the earth, and that it will destroy the people and the people's heritage. Maybe the naked Native American, and the other apparitions that have been encountered are really a warning to the people. Maybe they are trying to make contact or to instill a fear into people concerning what is being done to the land, and that maybe the cost is too great.

Checking on Mom

I went through a three-day safety class for a large company in Iowa about twenty years ago. The instructor, Robert, was a former Nebraska state patrol officer and a very personable man in his late forties. For good reason, he took his job as a safety trainer very seriously. Late into our second day of training it became pretty obvious to us that Robert had the gift of gab, and even enjoyed telling a joke now and then. As the day of training went on, the class started to close in on us. One of the students started a conversation with Robert, and soon the rest of the class was involved. Trying to keep him talking until the end of the day soon became the unspoken goal of the class.

Robert was full of stories about some of the ridiculous things he saw as a state patrol officer. There were stories about stupid criminals who forgot to fill their getaway cars with gas before going on a burglary spree. There were stories about disoriented elderly drivers and the silly excuses from teenagers when they were caught making out on deserted roads. Somehow the stories turned to drunk drivers, and Robert had a very elaborate and humorous list of excuses he had heard from intoxicated drivers when they were trying to convince him that they weren't drunk. Then Robert stopped.

He looked at the floor as he stood in front of us and didn't say anything for a couple of minutes. His voice began to tremble as he started to speak in a very somber voice we hadn't seen from him. About nine years prior, he was working the night shift in the Omaha area. At around 1:30 a.m., the dispatcher notified him of a two-car motor vehicle accident with injuries on a rural road. Robert was actually quite close to the location, so he notified dispatch that he was en route and asked if there was any more information about the accident. The dispatcher replied just that the caller was frantic, and she would relay as soon as she could get anything else out of the caller. He requested that fire and ambulance be paged if they hadn't already been notified.

About seven minutes later, Robert was on the scene. There was a full-sized pickup truck pointing up out of the left side of the ditch with heavy front-end damage, and what was left of a mid-sized sedan located in the middle of the road directly in front of the cruiser. The first person Robert talked to as he climbed out of his cruiser was a woman who lived about half a block away and called 911 after hearing what must have been a massive impact. She was screaming for help, and it was then that Robert could see the situation. The husband of the woman was restraining the driver of the truck, who was trying to run away, but was so intoxicated he almost couldn't stand up.

What was once a very beautiful teenage girl was lying face-down on the pavement in a pool of blood. Her mother was still in the seat of the car that her daughter had been ejected from. Robert called dispatch on his handheld and tried to stay calm as he asked to please hurry the ambulance, and confirmed at least two very serious casualties. At that time, a county car arrived on the scene. Robert pointed to the drunk driver, and the officer immediately detained him. Robert got down to check the young girl for a pulse and any signs of breathing. She was torn up badly and there were no vitals. With the damage that was done to her small body, it was obvious there was nothing he could do for her.

Her mom was barely hanging on, so Robert and the deputy tried to keep her as stable as they could until the ambulance arrived. As fire personnel arrived and began to disentangle the mother from the car, Robert returned to his cruiser to get a blanket to cover the now-confirmed deceased girl. He covered her up and walked back to the car to see if he could help with the mother. He was having a hard time because he was taking this accident too personally. He looked back at the body of the poor girl as he guided the cables for the fireman aligning the jaws to cut the car open.

To his horror, he saw the teenage girl lying in the road on her stomach with her head propped in her hands. Her elbows were on the pavement and it looked as if she were a young girl watching television. Her lips were moving, but he couldn't hear what she was saying over the noise of the engines and the jaws, but she was looking right at him. He tapped the firefighter on the shoulder and indicated he was going to the girl.

Robert ran to her and sat down on one knee and said, "What is it honey?"

She said in a weak voice, "Where's my mommy? I want my mommy."

"We are getting her out of there, honey. We are going to help her," he replied.

"Oh. Okay," she said. Robert rested his hand on her back and could feel bones popping as she laid her head back down on the pavement.

Robert began to choke up as he told us, "She was cold. She was dead. She was confirmed dead by the paramedic." The room went quiet for more than a few moments.

One of the students who I'm sure was just trying to lighten the mood a bit asked Robert, "How long have you been teaching these classes, because you sure do a great job of it."

He looked up at us with a troubled look and replied, "About nine years."

The Accident

Kevin became an instant friend of mine when we started working together. I gave him his driving test for the semi and even recommended him for a job to haul water in the oilfields of North Dakota. He is a Lakota, always has a smile on his face, and is just a pleasure to be around. I told him when he started his training that if he ever needed anything, or just needed to talk, he could call or come to see me and it would be my pleasure to help him in any way I could. On September 15, 2011, he took me up on my offer.

Kevin had just loaded his first load of the day, some production water. The weather was nearly perfect. He was heading north in the Mandaree area and was following two other trucks from another company. Kevin was following about half a mile behind the truck in front of him when he hit a bump in the road. He checked his mirrors to make sure that everything was fine, and when he looked back to the road he saw the first of the two trucks cross over the centerline with dust and debris flying into the air. Unsure of what happened, Kevin began to slow down. Both of the trucks in front of him stopped so Kevin eased up to them and stopped too. He got out and went to check that the other drivers were okay. Once he got to the first truck, he saw what happened.

There was a small pickup truck in the ditch with what appeared to be the driver partially ejected from the vehicle in an unnatural and grotesque position. Kevin told the other drivers that he was CPR certified and asked whether there was anyone else in the car. The first driver, who had apparently hit the pickup truck, kept repeating that the driver of the pickup truck was drinking.

Kevin made his way to the wreckage when the second truck driver stopped him and demanded, "What are you going to do? What story are you going to tell?"

Kevin said, "Hey man. I just want to see if there is anything I can do to help." The driver again asked why, and Kevin realized the other drivers were willing to get violent, but Kevin kept pushing them to let him get to the wreckage because he was certain that someone might need help. While Kevin was trying to persuade the drivers to let him go to the injured driver, a wildlife officer saw the accident and stopped, along with another driver from the company Kevin worked for, and they all went to the pickup. The female driver was dead, as well as a man in the passenger seat and a young boy no more than six or seven years old. The family dog had also died in the accident and was lying in the backseat. The wildlife officer was tearing up and asked Kevin if he would help get the bodies out. They went back to the officer's truck to get some gloves when they heard a horrible scream from the smashed truck. Oddly, it sounded like it came from the dog.

Kevin went back to the truck and found that the dead dog seemed to have moved. His paw was now on top of the head of a baby girl they had failed to see in the initial inspection, and she was still alive. They worked fast to get her out, but she was in very bad shape with blood coming from her mouth and nose. After they rescued the little girl from the car, the tribal police and ambulance were on the scene. After

Kevin gave his report to the officer, he left the scene to take the load of water to disposal and continue on with his job.

After driving for a few miles, the reality of the accident hit Kevin so hard that he had to pull over and stop his truck. He was struggling with the baby girl and the rough shape she was in. Her whole family was gone, and Kevin started to shake so badly that he couldn't drive. His dispatch had heard what happened and what he had been through, so they told him to go home and to get some rest, but Kevin couldn't get that baby girl out of his mind.

That night as he lay in bed he stared at the ceiling for a long time until he finally gave in to sleep. He was awakened in the middle of the night by something nudging his pillow. He didn't see anything so he closed his eyes to go back to sleep when something nudged the pillow again. This time Kevin rolled over to see the mom, dad, and young boy from the accident scene. Kevin wasn't scared or threatened by them, and he rolled over and wept.

I called Kevin the following day to ensure he was doing okay after I heard about the accident. As he started to tell me the story, I could feel a lump forming in my throat. Like him, I wanted to pack my bag and go home to my family so I could hold them in my arms for as long as I could, but I had to stay strong for Kevin. The gruesomeness of this story shook us both up. After talking to Kevin, I started to think about the situation. I thought about the bravery of the family dog, whose last attempt at life was to make sure that Kevin knew there was a baby girl in the car and she was still alive. I thought about the family appearing next to Kevin's bed that night, just looking at him. And I thought of the little girl, who eventually succumbed to her injuries and passed away as well the next morning.

I told Kevin that I believed the dog knew he was there to help, and gave his last bit of energy to help his girl. The family standing next to his bed was to thank him for being brave and not giving up until the very end, and saving the only piece of the family that survived. That little girl was cared for until the end of her life. Kevin is still struggling to deal with the events surrounding this accident, but in time I'm sure he will learn to cope with the pain of knowing how selfish some people can be, and how thankful some can be, either dead or alive, when you have done everything in your power to help them.

Into the Storm

The summer of 1983 was a very busy one. I was seventeen years old and following my dream of becoming an over the road truck driver, which was also the business I grew up with. Growing up in the family business had its burdens. As the owner's son, I had to work a little harder than everyone else and be a little more dedicated because I was determined not to be the typical boss's son.

In those days, many young men got their driving experience before they were of legal driving age, being taught how to operate the family machinery responsibly and safely by their fathers or grandfathers.

"It's our name on the door, and by God, you had better represent it like a man," my father used to remind me. Drugs, booze, and girl chasing were left to the dirt bags. We worked hard, very hard, and had beautiful equipment to prove it. We ran with other truckers who thought like we did. We wanted to get to the coast with our precious loads of dressed beef, reload, and get back home to our family as quickly as we could so we can do it all over again.

I was trying my hardest to be like those guys during that summer. I was working in the shop, changing oil, and polishing chrome. When we had time we were adding more and more lights to our truck, making them a recognizable rolling wall of illumination cutting through the darkness. The only thing missing was my dad, who had lost his battle with cancer eight years before. Luckily though, I had a friend, Ronnie, who taught me everything he knew about trucks, which included going on several runs with him to both coasts, hauling everything from lettuce to meat. He made sure I had more than enough time behind the wheel before I would go on my own to make sure that I was really ready. I have an amazing list of experiences from traveling with Ronnie in those days, but there is one that sticks out even now as just plain unexplainable.

Truck drivers are expected to go wherever the load is needed, and Brooklyn, New York, is no exception, and Ronnie let me take the wheel from our departure factory in Nebraska. As we got closer to the city late on a Sunday night, the trucks that we had been running with started to exit the freeway for their various destinations, and we were left alone to complete the final few hours to our stop. We parked along a side street outside of the locked fence where our delivery would be unloaded the next morning, and sat in the front seats talking and trying to keep each other awake to stay safe. We were unloaded at nine a.m., and Ronnie decided we should stop for something to eat. Knowing New York City quite well, Ronnie went into a grocery store and got the best sub sandwich I have ever had. He then told me we were heading to Philly to pick up a load that needed to be in Chicago in three days. This is an 850-mile trip, so even though it was good news that we would be leaving the East Coast so quickly, we were already exhausted and would have to drive like madmen to make the delivery on time. As it goes with the trucking industry, if we turned this load down we could sit for two days without work, so we decided to take on the challenge.

While we were loading in Philadelphia, Ronnie went in to deal with the load and I tried to get some sleep in the truck, which was tricky because the truck was being bounced around by the forklift going in and out of the trailer to load the seafood. Surprisingly, they had the trailer loaded and ready to go in less than two hours. We set our course for Chicago, and Ronnie told me to try and get some sleep so I could drive later. Sleep was almost impossible, however, because the roads were so rough.

Ronnie was able to go more than halfway before the caffeinated drinks just wouldn't work anymore. In Ohio he told me that he couldn't go any further, gave me directions to where we were headed, and we switched seats. I was tired and a little nervous, but I plugged in my favorite cassette tape, turned up the CB radio, and found a groove for a while.

When I crossed into Indiana, I drove into a pretty rough thunderstorm that brought hail, wind, and sometimes even zero visibility. There was a line of cars behind me using my lights as a guide to follow, which was quite a burden for a seventeen-year-old to think about. After the storm passed, I started to relax a bit and began to speed up a little to make up for the time I thought we had lost. The radio started to irritate me, so I turned it off. Shortly after that I started to struggle to stay awake.

We had green lights under the dash in the truck that lit up the floor so that we could easily see anything on the floor in the dark. I could see my Van Halen tape, a can of soda, and a pair of feet in the empty passenger seat. There was a pair of feet attached to legs. They were bouncing in the seat right next to me in time with the bumps on the highway. I nearly jumped out of my skin when they vanished as quickly as they had appeared. This incident shocked me right awake.

At that very second a voice came over the two-way radio asking for the green Pete heading westbound. To this I replied, "Go ahead." He told me to slow it way down because the storm had damaged some road signs in a construction zone and to quickly get into the left lane. I did as this man said, and within seconds saw a lighted sign that had been blown into a hole that I would have surely driven into. Possibly even killing both Ronnie and me in the process.

After my pulse came back down to a normal pace, I started to think about what had just happened. I realized I never saw the trucker who gave me the road report, and at three a.m., how did he know our truck was green? Then I started to think about what I had seen in the passenger seat seconds before the radio message. Was this fatigue, or an apparition?

I was still trying to make sense of it when I realized that whatever or whoever I saw was wearing exactly the same shoes and pants that my father always wore. In some way, maybe it was my father making sure I learned my lesson on how far to push myself before risking too much. No matter what the explanation, after that night I always knew what my limits were and when I was pushing them too far.

The Prairie School

Working as a driver for a large grocer can be a very fun job if your mind is in the right place. It can also be challenging delivering anywhere from seven to thirty stops a day to places like country clubs, public schools, institutions, and even high-end restaurants. There were benefits to this work, as well. Drivers were usually paid higher than average, they got to know a variety of people, and the job helped to keep the drivers in great physical shape because they had to unload every box on the truck with just the aid of basic delivery tools. This job can be fun, and the driver can get the inside scoop on the best places to eat, the toughest places to deliver, and in some cases, the most haunted places to deliver as well.

The late summer of 1991 was busy for Jessie. This was mainly because his route went right through Cheyenne, Wyoming, where their annual Frontier Days celebration was in full swing. Traffic was an issue when Jessie was trying to navigate his semi truck around the alleys and side streets to deliver his normal stops, because they all ordered twice the amount of groceries as they normally did. Not only did he have to deliver to his usual drops, but he had a delivery for Frontier Park too. He had huge orders of corn dogs and turkey legs that had to be manually wheeled to portable cold storage for the shady customers that he didn't like to deal with. This was doubly complicated because these were cash on delivery orders, so he had the burden of dealing with payments as well. On this particular day, Jessie got an unwanted surprise on his route. Not only did he have to deal with the added nuisance of the Frontier Days deliveries, but now he also had to go an hour out of his way to a tiny town for a delivery to a small public school.

Jessie loved the people at the school, but he wished they would have waited another week for their order to get the rush of Frontier Days out of the way. Not only did he have to drive two hours round-trip to make this delivery, he had to be there between twelve and twelve-thirty in the afternoon or the person meeting him at the school would close it and he couldn't make the delivery. He pulled in with ten minutes to spare and drove around to the parking lot, but didn't see a single car parked at the school. Being a town of only a couple hundred people, Jessie thought maybe whoever was suppose to meet him at the school may have walked there, so he went to the door and knocked. The door opened as if it wasn't closed all the way. He looked into an audio/visual room and an entrance to what looked to be the auditorium with a stage and closed curtain.

Jessie yelled into the building, "Is anyone here?" He immediately heard someone walk across the stage. It sounded like a woman in high heels, but no one answered his call.

He shouted again. "Hello!" Still, no response. He knew someone was in there, so he decided to walk to the stage and see if he could see who he heard walking. He walked into the room, walked up the steps, and pulled the curtain back to look at the stage area. No lights were on and it was very hard for Jessie to see. He did make a note that the stage had a hardwood floor, so that would explain the loud footsteps he had heard.

Getting agitated at the time he was losing, he yelled again a little louder. "Grocery delivery." Again, there was no answer. *This is great*, Jessie thought. *Losing three hours for thirty cases of canned goods.*

He walked back outside, pulled the door closed, which locked behind him, and went to his truck to wait a few more minutes. At 12:55 p.m., Jessie started his truck and was preparing to head back to continue on his route. Just when he was getting ready to leave, a small pickup pulled into the parking lot and a woman jumped out. She was immediately very apologetic, and explained that she had lost track of time and was sorry she had cost him time.

Jessie was relieved because he wanted them to get their order, so he hurriedly opened the trailer and had her canned goods unloaded as quickly as possible. While the woman was checking in her order, Jessie asked if she was the only one at the school that day.

To this she giggled and said, "Oh my yes. School doesn't start for another two weeks or so." Jessie asked her if there were janitors or anyone else who could be in the building. "Nope, just me," she replied, but then stopped and looked up at him and asked why. It was almost as if she knew what he was going to say.

He explained to her what he had heard on the stage, and suggested he wasn't comfortable leaving her there by herself because he was sure of what he had heard earlier.

She gave him a very big smile, handed Jessie his signed delivery slip and said, "Don't you worry about me. This happens from time to time."

On the drive to his next delivery, Jessie started to question himself why he didn't ask her to explain what she meant. He got the impression that those high heels he heard on the stage at that little public school was just a part of everyday life there. The surrounding towns are all known to have interesting residents, so there's no telling if this high heeled visitor was the only thing that comes to this school, or if there are others that frequent this space as well.

chapter three

Weird Places

The stories are everywhere. All you have to do is take the time to sit down and listen to them. We have to turn down our stressed-out, twenty-first century brains and listen. The stories about those who find themselves all alone in the back country trailing cattle, or driving through the desert in the early morning, or those in the middle of a vacation who find an area that just doesn't feel right. It's those times when your horse or dog will not move, their ears pointed straight back with a severe case of animal apprehension, sensing something we can't even begin to feel or understand. Then there are those who are especially sensitive to their surroundings when the hair on the back of their neck stands up, and the instruments they have been relying on for months are suddenly acting weird.

The stories and locations that follow in this chapter are very real, but some are more notorious than others. Some could be right in your backyard, and some you can only imagine what it would be like to be in. It could be a trail that you have traveled on several times before, but is now different in some weird way. You could even start to get the feeling that you are not alone. We try to use logic to explain these instances away and convince ourselves we are just being foolish. But weird things happen in these weird places.

The Magnetic Fields

My grandfather used to tell me stories many years ago about a place that he used to refer to as the magnetic fields. It was in a little-known part of western Iowa near a town called Atlantic, and as a child, a town on the edge of the Great Plains with a name like that seemed like enough of a mystery for me. That is until after a vacation in 1977 when a strange event occurred with our CB radio in the vicinity of the magnetic fields. My grandfather decided then to explain what had happened to him in that area when he was just a young man working to help his mother put food on the table for the rest of his family.

I was somewhat of a two-way radio nerd in the 1970s and received my FCC license when I was eleven, sort of a big deal at a time when you had to actually test out to become a CB radio operator. I loved scanning the channels and following weather patterns to see how far I could send the 7-watt AM carrier off of a mobile unit. I had pretty good success at long-distance communication, even though I had to keep reaffirming that I was indeed a boy when my radio voice sounded more like a teenage girl, which made things difficult for me on the channel mostly used by truckers.

On an early July morning in 1977, while following a semi truck in our Ford Galaxy, something happened that I still can't explain while monitoring the trucker channel. It was business as usual for the truckers that morning. I was listening to repeated weather reports and we had just driven through a thunderstorm, so that was what our conversation was revolving around. We were about ten miles from the magnetic fields and communication with other stations became impossible. A very strong carrier with something that sounded like boiling water being amplified through a PA system was all we could get to come through. It was constant and very irritating. We couldn't get anything else for more than twenty miles.

At first I thought it was because of the thunderstorm, but then I thought that maybe there was an issue with our radio and got upset that I would have to go the remainder of the ride to Colorado without my CB radio. When we pulled into an Omaha gas station, truckers who were a few miles behind us started to come in and tell the trucks going the opposite direction about the weird things happening on the radio. It was a mystery to everyone that heard it.

After we returned home to Iowa, I explained to my grandfather what had happened and where it happened. "That doesn't surprise me at all," he replied. He wasn't a radio buff, but he was very familiar with the area.

My great-grandfather all but abandoned his family in 1927. Being a responsible young man, my grandfather decided to set out from his home and try to generate an income for his siblings and help out his mother in any way that he could. Grandpa was a self-taught mechanic, farrier, farmer, and official witcher of water. He used all of his strengths and talents to make whatever money he could. At one point, his travel brought him to the area of the magnetic fields. While farming, Grandpa told of a very strange occurrence with a team of horses while plowing an enormous plot just south of the fields.

"The damn horses just froze," he explained. "They just froze. Their ears pointed straight back and their eyes showed fear as both of them started to snort and paw at the soil as if they were going to charge something." Grandpa was afraid that he was about to lose control of the two tons of horseflesh that he was responsible for, and reined them back a little while speaking softly and gently to them, even though his own hair was standing straight up.

"I was scared," Grandpa said while striking the table. He was eighteen years old and couldn't afford to mess up. Losing a draft team of this quality would have surely cost him his job and any pay he would have been expecting. The horses heeded Grandpa's soothing voice and held their position with great apprehension. They refused to move, and Grandpa wasn't going to push the issue, so he just stood there looking for the source of what had spooked his team so badly. Of course, there was no evidence of anything out of line other than the horrible feeling of fear and the overwhelming urge to run as fast as he could for the barn.

He knew he wasn't imagining it because his team was in a near panic. Grandpa thought it was at least a couple hours before his and the horses's apprehension eased enough to get moving again. He finished as the sun dropped below the horizon, and he still had to get the team back to the barn, care for them, and put them up for the night. Once he completed his jobs, he knew he would have to explain his poor productivity for the day. Over dinner that evening, he explained to his boss what had happened with the horses and the feeling of fear that he felt.

The farmer replied, "Yes. I know all about that," and that was the end of the conversation.

After the plowing and planting jobs were done, my grandfather's new duty was to find possibilities for a well on the land bordering where the horses had been spooked. My grandfather was an expert at finding productive locations for a well, and I am proud to have that passed down to me from him. One day, however, something threw a little wrench in his water-finding wheel.

Grandpa was creeping out along the land but had very few hits on his witching rod. He thought the land was water-rich based on his experience, but the instruments were not responding the way he thought they would. Fear came over him suddenly and the instruments went berserk. He said it was like playing tug-of-war with an invisible opponent. The switch pulled violently toward the sky, to the left, and to the right, but never toward the ground, which is where it should have pointed. He had never experienced anything like this before. He struggled with it for a few seconds and then let go of the switch, which flew away from him and went several yards. It landed on the ground at the approximate area where the horses had been spooked a few weeks earlier. This time he said nothing to the boss.

Grandpa was cutting through the area on a beautiful July day. He was walking through the cornfield, carrying his favorite basket to the far side of the field in search of mulberries and some dandelion greens for dinner. It was a great day to watch the fruits of your labor mature in the Iowa soil, when the damned magnetic fields struck again. It was a typical hot and humid July day, with no wind, but all of a sudden Grandpa's favorite basket was pulled from his hands. He stood there and watched as his basket went higher and higher into the sky, until it was out of sight, never to be seen again.

Soon after that, my grandpa hooked up with a harvest crew and ended up harvesting wheat in the Dakotas. After the harvest was done, he headed back south and to the comfort of his family's home to share the wealth of his labor and provide for his mother and siblings. We never heard an explanation of why things happened when we were in that area. But throughout my grandfather's life, he never forgot what had happened to him on that farm south of Atlantic during the 1920s.

A Life in Iowa, Along the River

Growing up in Iowa in the 1970s and '80s was really quite fun. We could ride our dirt bikes and three-wheelers along several miles of the heavily wooded Des Moines River north of Des Moines, resulting in nothing but fuel consumption and good memories. The Saylorville Reservoir was completed in the mid-1970s and offers visitors camping, beaches, fishing, trails, and picnic areas. When it was completed it hampered our long-distance ATV trips, but we still had great times there. Fourmile Creek, just northeast of Des Moines, was a hotspot for my friends, especially those who tubed the creek on the hot Iowa summer days. The skies somehow seemed unusually blue then. Most of the music was happy and positive, and we made the most of our childhood.

It may seem strange that these places could in any way fit into a category of weird places, but after reading these accounts from not that long ago, you may understand how some strange mysteries can exist right under our noses. Some of your daily commutes may pass right by these locations, not even commanding the smallest bit of your interest as you go about your everyday lives. Some of these stories may give you a reason to take a second glance and bring a smile across your face thinking about what happened there.

Not even a generation ago the area along the Des Moines River was very different from the way it is today. Independent country people who endured floods, tornadoes, animals, and intruders occupied little shacks built along the river. Trapping, fishing, and bootlegging were great ways to boost personal income in those areas. Even up to a few years ago, there were still a few families who didn't have indoor plumbing, and they were still running illegal trap lines, producing corn liquor, and coon hunting, but they are all gone today. As a child, I came to like these river dwellers, but knew my boundaries and didn't ask questions about the copper kettle behind the shed, or the number of pelts nailed to the wall. When these people realized that I meant them no harm, they started to talk and I would listen. Their knowledge of survival and instincts can't even compare to anyone else I have ever met in my life. I always knew that if I ever needed anything from the people I met at the river, they would do whatever they could, and I always hoped they felt the same about me.

By the time I reached my teenage years, I knew where most of these people were, and knew that there were other areas that were hideouts for vagrants and those up to no good, and best left alone. One of the trail access sites was one of those places where kids didn't go alone. It even became a place to dump bodies in the late 1970s. My friend and his dad walked over one without knowing it until days later, when the smell of decay led the sheriff department to the scene. My friend never forgot that, and because of that one incident, we only went to that area on dirt bikes or ATVs. In later years, we were sure to carry some sort of protection with us too.

In the spring of 1983, my friend Alan and I decided to take advantage of an early dismissal from school and some unusually warm weather. We took my new three-wheeler and his new ATV to the river and rode north toward the Saylorville Reservoir. It was a great day, and because the leaves hadn't grown back on the trees yet, we could see things that we normally couldn't see in the summer with the overgrown land. There were a lot of muddy areas surrounded by walls of cottonwood, sycamore, and oak trees that were storm damaged and gnarled. We rode for about an hour and then stopped for a break. We found a trail that seemed to follow the river, although we couldn't see the river. It was getting late, and we thought we could follow the trail a ways before we loaded up to go home. The trail was barely wide enough for my three-wheeler and seemed to be a well-traveled trail and footpath. I knew the general area but after about ten minutes we were lost. The area's features changed as the sun started to dip behind the trees. Alan said that it felt like we were barricaded behind a wall of impenetrable trees. I was becoming nervous and felt responsible for Alan's safety, and I was failing him. I started to take note of some landmarks that would help, but our field of vision was less than 100 feet because of the undergrowth. I at least knew the river was to my right. I could smell the water; I just couldn't see it.

I laughed nervously and said to Alan, "I know where I am, but I don't know where I am." My sixteen-year-old mind was on overload as I estimated that we maybe had an hour of light left. We both had headlights on our vehicles, but we were lost during the day, so the headlights wouldn't help. We sure didn't want to be out there in the dark with our parents worrying about us. We climbed out of another mud hole that was fifty feet across onto a trail. We traveled another 100 yards and climbed up a very short, but very steep, hill in an area still surrounded by heavy tree growth. I made it up the hill, but Alan didn't. His ATV fell straight back on top of him about halfway up the climb. I ran down to see if he was hurt, and helped him and his machine up the hill. He was bruised, but okay.

At the top of the hill, we took another break to gather our senses and try to get the hell out of there. That's when I noticed my first real landmark. There was a 1950s Ford truck with its front end sticking straight up in the air and its bed mostly buried in soil from a flood years ago. I opened the hood out of curiosity and found an engine still in it. I told Alan I wanted to come back and get that engine, and we started our ATVs and continued on. After another 100 yards, we came upon a large horse barn and the foundation of a structure that looked to be a dance hall. I walked up a small flight of stairs to a large floor area with black and white tiles. We then checked out the barn, which was long abandoned, but decided to move on because it was quickly getting very dark.

I told Alan, "There's two landmarks. If we see them again, we know we are running in circles." We continued on using the light of our little headlights. We found ourselves on a road by the river and I became very disoriented about where we were. We illegally ran our machines back to our trucks and hoped if a police officer caught us they would understand what we had just been through.

A few days later we were hit with a terrible snowstorm that hampered our riding along the river for several weeks. Alan and I told our other friends about getting lost and finding the old truck and abandoned barn. We all agreed we needed to go back and try to find the area again so we could show all our buddies what we found. I also wanted that truck engine really bad and wanted to see if I could get my pickup truck close to it.

I mentioned our find to my grandfather, and he thought it was the same place he used to take my grandmother dancing. He thought it was called something like Sycamore Park. He told me of Saturday night gala events, and a ferry that would bring people to the park from the eastside of the river. He even described the black and white tiles on the dance floor. Now I was even more motivated and wanted to take a camera to get photos for my grandpa.

That fall my friends and I took my truck to the area and found none of my landmarks. We hiked to see what we could find on foot, but had no luck. It was a slow flood that year, and even if the barn was washed away, the dance floor should still be there. We finally gave up, but every year after that I would search on foot or in my truck for these structures. My future wife would even help me search, but we still had no results.

In 2005 we tried again. It was now illegal to ride ATVs in the area, so I waited for dark on an early October evening to unload my new ATV equipped with all the accessories, including a winch and a ton of lights. I let my family know where we were headed, and my wife and I went straight to where we wanted to start our search. The night was clear with a full moon as we followed a well-worn ATV trail with our lights flickering off of the trees. As we bounced along the trail and crawled further into the woods, we came to a depression of swampy water that we slowly went through. The area looked like a Louisiana swamp with eerie moonlight casting shadows across the vines and grisly looking trees. In my head, I figured that after the floods of 1983, and the more catastrophic flood of 1993, there most likely wasn't anything left of the barn, but the dance floor had to be there on its block foundation; even if it was partially covered by debris. As our four-wheeler chugged through the swamp and back up a small hill, my headlights shown on a much steeper climb up through the vines. I told my wife to hold on and we began up the hill with our headlights pointing straight up to the tops of the trees. As we crested the hill, our lights came back down and aimed directed at an old truck half buried in sludge. It was THE truck, and the engine was still in it!

I instantly got chills and told my wife, "I don't believe it! It's the truck!" We searched as well as we could in the dark, but never found that dance floor. We hiked the area the next day, but still with no luck. We just had the memories of getting lost and finding a piece of history that somehow vanished. It did give my friends and me a reason to search and think that, maybe someday, we will find the old area that is just not big enough to hide such a relic. But my story isn't the only strange thing that happened along this river.

A good friend of mine from childhood, Ed Gillman, grew up within a short distance of Fourmile Creek. Those were his stomping grounds, including muddy feet playing in the creek and riding his dirt bike with mud on the back. Although he, his friends, and his brothers knew the area quite well, Ed was very apprehensive of the areas across the creek that was heavily forested with pine and hardwood trees. While playing near the creek as a young child, Ed was terrified by an unbelievably loud scream coming from the trees across the creek. He instantly ran home and told his parents. He later told me it didn't sound human and was extremely loud. His parents just thought it was someone out in the trees being silly. Ed never forgot this incident, and several years later while he and a group of friends were riding tubes down the creek, he heard the noise again. Moving only as fast as the flow would take them, they heard two more screams during their trip. It was as if the creature that made this sound was following them. They told me the story a few weeks later, but I had no desire to go into these woods to investigate what it might have been.

Ed knew the area, and it had a reputation of having some well-known hermits living in the woods harvesting animals and going to houses at night to steal whatever they thought they needed. Despite this, Ed still could not figure out what could have been in the area for so many years trying to scare him and other people away.

In 1987 a friend of ours decided to ride a tube down the creek with some friends and encountered the same scream in the same spot. As he started telling people about it, more and more people admitted to hearing the same sound. Ed and his friends started to call the area "screaming valley." Other people from the area also know it as this, and all have some sort of strange story to go along with it. Stories include everything from the feeling of being followed to unexplainable lights moving among the trees. Other than the stories that have been passed down through families and generations, no explanation has ever come from what any of us experienced at this river.

The Four Corners

The area where Colorado, Utah, Arizona, and New Mexico come together is known as the Four Corners. There are not enough words to describe this unbelievable area, although many come to mind. This area is beautiful, lonely, peaceful, mysterious, dangerous, and haunted. This region is known worldwide for its rich archaeological and natural history, as well as its mysteries. From lost civilizations to runaway murderers who thought they could survive the elements and complicated geography of the area for the perfect hideout, the Four Corners area is full of the unexplained, and forever will be. For as long as there are storytellers, the region will keep supplying stories for every time there are lost people and disoriented hikers with no reasonable explanation for what they experienced or how they found their way out. Most of the stories are of ghosts and Native American legends; of skinwalkers and lights in the sky, as well as secret military bases and interdimensional portals that have led hikers and four-wheelers to areas forever lost. The stories are as old as man's existence in the region, and some are well recorded.

The story of the seven cities of gold is said to date back as far as 1150 AD. Spanish explorers carried rumors with them of gold-laden cities to the north of Mexico, fueled by confirmation by the Native Americans that they did indeed exist. The search began for the famed cities of gold in the late 1530s.

An early expedition led by Spanish priest Marcos De Niza began exploring the lands to the north. De Niza followed a guide named Estevanico, who he had sent ahead of him as a scout and to gather information. They made it as far as New Mexico before his death at the hands of the Zuni tribe. This may have caused Niza to turn back, but not before Niza saw a Zuni settlement called *hawikuh* from a distance, and claimed it appeared to be rich and well populated. His reports then led to the famous expedition, led by Francisco Vasquez de Coronado, in 1540.

These expeditions found no cities rich with gold and ended in great disappointment, and sometimes even in loss of life. The Spanish expeditions led to legends of lost or buried Spanish gold in southern Colorado and northern New Mexico. It is believed that some of the cities rumored to be the seven cities were not even inhabited at all. Those are the abandoned cities of the Anasazi in the Canyon de Chelly area in northern Arizona.

The ruins here carry with them great mystery as to who built them, why they were built in those specific areas, and why they were abandoned in the manner that they were. Evidence suggests that they were abandoned in a very quick fashion, with stocked granaries and pottery still in the dwellings, which were difficult to access because some of the ruins in precarious locations. Visitors almost need a knowledge of proper footing to even climb to the dwellings. It is almost like a password sequence to reach the ruins without falling off the cliff they are built on. There is evidence of farming, irrigation, and trade as far away as South America. Mummified parrots have been found in Anasazi burial sites, and Anasazi baskets and pottery have even been found in burial sites in southern Mexico.

During a college study in the early 1990s, a hypothesis was tested to prove that along the well-traveled trade routes south of the Four Corners travelers may have had help with night navigation. Evidence of ancient fire pits exists on top of select mesas within clear view of the paths below. Several fires were lit at these locations as the people below confirmed that they could indeed see the fires quite well, and they could be used to help find their way through a pitch-black, desert night.

Charles Wetherill accidentally discovered the most magnificent cliff dwellings in the area on December 18, 1888. He was a cowboy chasing strays when he came upon a chilling site that was basically an abandoned city, later called the Cliff Palace. This dwelling has 150 separate rooms, a large square tower, and no less than twenty-three ceremonial chambers, called *kivas*. It was later determined that the buildings originated in the late 1100s. More of these dwellings were discovered at Keet Seel in Arizona and Chaco Canyon in New Mexico. These are all magnificent locations to explore, and one never feels quite alone at these sites. Anyone who is sensitive to these things can feel the presence of ancient peoples while walking the paths and driving the lonely trails that abound in the canyons and mesas of the area. And without a doubt, over the last century the area has generated its share of unexplained events.

As I sat in the comfort of my truck, I thought to myself what a treacherous area it is. As I made my way down the canyon I glanced behind the passenger seat at the water and food supply that I brought with me, and tried to imagine how far I could stretch them if, heaven forbid, something should happen and I had to stay longer than planned due to some unforeseeable circumstance. Driving through the canyon, I realized how dependent we have become on the presence of other humans, which you don't notice until you are totally alone in a place like this. I tried to calm my apprehension by remembering that I built a reliable off-road truck, my ham radio was mounted in front of me, and my friend's truck was behind me. Only a fool would go into that area alone.

A Day Hike

My neighbor John took his family for a hike in the Canyonlands National Park in southeast Utah on a perfectly sunny day. Not being able to monitor the weather conditions from the bottom of the canyon, John decided it was time to guide his family back up and out of the area they were hiking in. He couldn't explain why he suddenly had the feeling that they needed to get out, but he knew it was time to go. He put his wife first in line and had their three children follow behind her in a single file line. John fell in line at the end, calmly prodding his family to move a little faster up the steep hiking trail.

John's calm feelings suddenly transformed into a sense of real danger as he kept after his tired kids to speed up. The top of the wash was still a few yards ahead of them when a cool rush of air hit John and his family. He knew full well what that meant and yelled at his family to run. When John's wife reached the top, she turned and grabbed the children. As John grabbed the youngest child and threw him to his wife, a twenty-foot wall of red water, along with logs riding the crest like a bizarre surfer, rushed into the canyon right in the area that they had been. The noise was deafening as John leapt for the top of the trail and into safety as his wife grabbed his hands to pull him over. The flash flood would surely have killed his entire family if they had stayed for one more second on their climb out of the wash. Thankfully, for some unexplainable instinctual fear, John's family was untouched and only his feet were wet. It was that close.

As he caught his breath, John noted that there were some dark clouds with rain tails about twenty-five miles upstream, and above them was a hot, blistering late-afternoon sun and crystal clear skies. There were no visible reasons for the water and logs to crest over the canyon. It was as if it came out of nowhere, just as John's feelings came out of nowhere.

The Treasure Hunters

I can remember hearing stories of treasure seekers in the 1940s and '50s, armed with notes and hand-drawn maps, to sites that they thought were lost Spanish gold mines or caches with valuable coins and artifacts. Some of these adventurers were never to be seen again, while others would return days later than expected, armed with bizarre tales of being lost in an area with lush vegetation and humid air, and the mules that would refuse to move at the very spot the environment changed. They would search and search for anything familiar, with no luck. Then suddenly the area would change back to something familiar and the treasure hunters could safely return home. They would come with no treasure and no desire to ever return to the mesas and canyons of the Four Corners ever again, for any amount of money.

I have come in contact with experienced backpackers. They are a hardy group of individuals who see every square inch of the areas they travel to. These are not the daytime hikers who casually travel our favorite trails. These are seasoned backpackers who travel and survive in these places for weeks. They take a great amount of time to expertly learn about their destinations months ahead of time. They research the history, weather, topography, and flora and fauna of the area and adjust themselves and their gear accordingly. What some of them couldn't research and prepare for was the possibility of a brush with the unknown.

There are stories about flickering lights on top of mesas that sit hundreds of feet above the ancient trails used by the Anasazi more than 900 years ago. Could these be signal fires still burning? There are also constant reports of unidentified lights in the sky that seemingly follow night hikers trying to get back to their vehicles at the end of their stay.

The Navajo, who are native to this area, know better than to disturb or even visit the ruins of the ancient people. They believe that the dead are best left alone, and the fear of an encounter with the *chindi* (the ghost left behind after a person dies), who would for sure bring some sort of misfortune or even death, is not worth the risk.

The Skinwalker

The Navajo legend of skinwalkers is one of the most terrifying, and filled with the most mystery. The tribe believes powerfully in this legend, but refuses to discuss it or any sightings with other people for fear of what may happen. The legend states that a walker is a tribe member who obtains the highest level of power in the tribe, but uses their powers for evil rather than for good. Therefore, they are able to transform into an animal that will allow them to inflict pain and harm on others. They are typically seen as a coyote, owl, fox, wolf, or crow, but are able to turn into any animal.

I remember attending a barbecue in Colorado in 2007 when the conversation turned to Highway 666 in southeast Utah for some reason. One young man spoke up and explained why he would never return to that area again. Growing up on a ranch on the border of Utah and Colorado this young man was very grounded and realistic, and growing up in this lonely area can erase any mystery of being in the wild, but in the fall of 1996 that changed forever.

As he and two friends were on their way to New Mexico for a high school basketball game, they noticed they were being followed … by a half man, half wolf entity on the Ute Mountain Reservation land. In a panic they tried to outrun the horrifying creature, but couldn't until they neared the lights of a truck stop. They stopped under the lights of the fuel station to catch their breath, and even considered calling the authorities until they realized that nobody would believe a word of their story. It took many years for any of them to even start to tell their story, and even in 2008 were still very careful who they told it to.

There are countless stories from people who have had similar experiences with skinwalkers, but most are reluctant to share their stories. Any mention of these creatures makes locals skittish and invokes fear in the area of any sightings.

The Fugitives

Any story about any Four Corners phenomenon would be incomplete without talking about who are known as the "Four Corner Fugitives." I am brought back to the end of May 1998. Three men went on a theft and killing rampage beginning in Cortez, Colorado. The crime spree started when the men stole a large water truck, brutally killed a local police officer, and wounded another officer and a number of observers. The men eventually ditched the water truck and stole another vehicle before vanishing into the Cross Canyon of the Four Corners, outfitted with large caches of food, water, and ammunition.

Hundreds of law enforcement officers converged on the area to assist in finding these three madmen. After coming up empty-handed, the search started to wind down with life getting back to normal. Reports would occasionally come in on possible sightings and from law enforcement being fired upon by, who they assumed, were the fugitives. Still, no one was able to find them. Soon, the fugitive's bodies were discovered, one by one.

The first was discovered after a man was fired at after stopping by a local river for a picnic. Authorities rushed to the area and found a man with a bullet hole in his head. Officers ruled it a suicide, but the official documents stated the cause of death as undetermined. A year and a half after the original killing spree, some Navajo deer hunters stumbled upon human bones. The surrounding area was identical to what they found near the first body so officials knew they had another one. This death was also ruled as a suicide, but officials argued this as well. So far, they had two fugitives dead of what should have been looked at as suicide, but the ringleader was still at large.

Not until 2007 did the case finally come to a close. A cowboy on horseback in the area saw what he thought was a blanket on the ground. It turned out to be a bulletproof vest and human bones. This one also had a gunshot to the head, and was the final fugitive. The manhunt ended here, but the story is far from over.

There has never been a clear motive for what prompted these three men to go on a rampage and want to disappear into the desert. They had enough food and supplies to survive for up to three years in the canyons, but they didn't make it that far. Many stories say that the men were all dead within a few days of the initial crimes, but no one can know for sure. Not only that, but the stories surrounding their deaths still remains a mystery as well. The real reason why their lives ended the way they did will probably forever be hidden among the junipers, rocks, and caves of Cross Canyon.

The Ancient Ones

It is hard to even imagine a place like this if you haven't been there to experience it. I have endured decades of travel in this area, and every trip is full of new experiences. As the darkness of night began to swallow up the surrounding canyon walls, I slowed my truck a rough and dusty mile away from our intended campsite. I looked around in absolute awe at the unbelievable and impossible landscape I got to travel through. Only the occasional chirp of my tires on the slick rocks reminded me that I was indeed still in the twenty-first century, and to turn on the radio to distract from this view would be a sin. As the darkness thickened around us we plodded on, and I couldn't help the overwhelming feeling of being watched or followed as I turned on my off-road lights, and tried to stay focused on the trail ahead and not on the mesa tops above us, no matter how badly I felt the urge to scan the ridges above me for whatever I felt looking down on us.

I followed the trail up and out of the wash we had been plodding in for the better part of two hours, and my hood was pointing straight up in the air. My lights were illuminating the dust in the air well above the cliff that was right in front of me. As my truck leveled out again, into an area of deep sand, my lights caught a massive petroglyph that had to have been left by the Fremont people, who inhabited the area more than 1,200 years ago. The petroglyph was at least fifteen feet up the side of the cliff, and at least fifteen feet high. It was human in shape, but otherworldly in design. It was created in rust-colored hues, and as I stopped to study it while waiting for my friend, I noticed something that still has a profound effect on me. There was an outline of a human hand on the cliff, much smaller than mine. I accept this as a direct communication with someone who left this plane centuries ago.

A warm and almost spiritual feeling came over me as I stood in from of my truck, and any fears and apprehensions left me as I noticed that I was casting a perfect shadow of myself on the cliff in front of me. As I wondered who that person could have been: a lonely hunter, a tribal leader, or a medicine man, I placed the shadow of my hand directly over the tracing. It was like a peaceful greeting from my world to his, and while listening to the purr of my idling truck behind me, I got the strongest feeling that he was here somewhere. Either in the air, or the rock, raising his hand to mine.

This truly is a most wonderful place.

The Mutilators

Stories of animal mutilations have been reported all over the country for more than fifty years. There has never been an arrest, witness, or explanation to any of the instances. If any arrest was ever made, it has the potential to be the story of the century; damages would reach millions of dollars, and people in the livestock industry would sleep a lot better not having to worry about their animals. In our crazy world, we have gotten used to stories of alleged conspiracies and mysterious hidden agendas from corporate companies or gov-

ernment entities. There has yet t[...]
of these disturbing instances, but [...]
body out there knows something[...]
best we can get for now.

The first documented report [...]
ferred to as animal mutilation was i[...]
rado. A horse nicknamed Snippy v[...]
dead in a pasture. Her skin and flesh [...]
the shoulders and head, with the heart and brain removed.
There were no tracks near the body and no blood on the
ground. The horse's owners recalled a flattened bush, ex-
haust marks, and strange indentations in the ground near
the site.

This was exactly the mystery the press and the public
were searching for. Remember that by this time, people
were very well-informed about the UFO phenomenon, and
this type of an event seemed to tie right into it. It created
some new and very interesting hypotheses tying both mysteries together in a twist of confusion and assumptions.

Following the Snippy mystery, it seemed like almost every dead food-stock animal found in a field in an unusual
way became a mutilation, whether it indeed was or not. Although there have been many reports of actual animal mutilations, not every death could be ruled as such. Those who
did not grow up on a ranch or farm or had little experience
with livestock would be more inclined to believe the more
sensational stories. However, not all events can be explained
away so easily.

firsthand contact with the cattle mutilation was as a teenager in the 1980s. There had been re- in Iowa of a reported cattle mutilation that I had been ollowing when I happened to talk to a man who owned some property in the Colorado foothills where his family had run cattle. They got out of the cattle business in 1981 and leased their land to another rancher who ran cattle and also kept a large string of lease horses on the property. It wasn't long before problems started, and a pair of cattle ended up dead. It was a cow and calf pair. The cattle had been horribly mutilated and left to rot on the hillside where the bodies were found. The rancher told the property owner what had happened and kept an open ear to the problem. Investigation of the location and the state of the carcasses actually leaned toward cult activity that law enforcement officers were already aware of, but they produced no suspects.

The rancher was understandably very upset at his loss, and started to take the law into his own hands by patrolling the property with loaded rifles. He just wasn't sure what or who he was searching for. The cattle had been found a considerable distance from the access road to the property, and there were no signs of struggle from either animal. In fact, they were lying right next to each other, which seemed strange no matter what the cause of death was. There was never a definitive perpetrator or cause found for the death of these animals, but due to the state that they were found, it can be ruled as some sort of animal mutilation.

Fast-forward to 1995, and I am transporting bulk salt to beef packers, and bulk feeds to dairy farms and cattle feeding operations in Colorado, Nebraska, and Utah with my family. While having a conversation with one of our regular customers in Colorado, I was told the following story, which was tragic to the rancher and his family. If there was ever anyone that I regularly contacted in those days of my work and someone who sincerely loved his animals, it was this man. He and his family had a cattle operation on the eastern plains of Colorado, and they were very dedicated and caring to the animals that were under their care.

One evening in the mid-1980s, he noticed that his string of horses seemed rattled, and was gathered up by the fence line next to the barn. It was early spring, and he couldn't see a reason why the horses would be so upset. His favorite gelding, however, was not with the herd. The rancher chirped and whistled a few times to see if he could call him, but he didn't see the horse anywhere. He could hear cattle bawling out in the distance and guessed that coyotes were in the area, even though his sons had taken care of a few of them the previous week.

He went into the house for supper, but finished quickly because he was concerned about his gelding. After he was done eating, he turned on a floodlight on the back porch of his house and strained to see the horses. They were still milling about by the fence, had their backs turned to him, and still seemed out of sorts, with their ears pointing straight back. Right at this point, another mare came storming out of the darkness, all frothed up kicking and snorting. But still there was no gelding. He grabbed his oldest son and their rifles, and got into their truck to search.

They drove out into the dark through the gate and into the rolling hills. They drove around for almost an hour, but didn't see the gelding. The man started to feel sick to his stomach, and had the feeling he would never see his horse again. Having no luck, the two checked all the immediate fences before returning to the house.

At the first sight of sunlight the following morning, the man grabbed his rifle and jumped in his truck to return to the range looking for his horse. Within a few minutes, his fear was realized as he saw his gelding lying dead about a quarter-mile away from the house. The rest of the animals wouldn't go within 300 feet of the animal and were visibly shaken. He jumped out of his truck and laid his hand on his old friend as he wiped tears from his cheek. After the initial shock of finding his favorite horse dead, the rancher realized that something was quite wrong with the scene. He said that he noticed an odd chemical smell similar to formaldehyde. All four legs of the gelding looked to be broken, the flesh on half of his face was missing, upon closer inspection, he noticed that the animal's anus looked to have been cut out, and there was a small opening in the horse's chest. Not only that, but there was no blood, no sign of struggle, and no tire or human tracks at the site other than his own. It even looked like the horse had been dropped there somehow. He couldn't find any tracks in the soft soil that the horse had even walked to that spot. The rancher lived on this property and had seen several incidents of predators and attacks on calves from coyotes and the occasional mountain lion, but this was very different.

After the man reported the incident to the authorities, a deputy arrived to have a look in early afternoon. While on a hill overlooking the location of the dead horse, both men noticed that no predatory animals seemed to have taken interest in the carcass yet. It seemed strange, given the fact that raw flesh was exposed on the facial wound, which should have attracted animals from miles away. The deputy took some pictures and shared that he had seen this type of incident before, and outright called it a mutilation. This immediately upset the rancher because it now took on the characteristics of a criminal trespass, and quite literally the murder of his favorite horse. He and his family couldn't think of who would do such a thing.

This event was the beginning of several months of patrolling the ranch with loaded rifles to make sure it never happened again. No reasonable explanation was ever given, and the rancher never notified any press. They weren't that kind of people and didn't want to draw extra attention to the area. The rancher did indicate that in the day preceding the killing, they heard what sounded like an abnormal amount of aircraft in the area after dark. They specifically heard more helicopter traffic. As gruesome and unimaginable as this seems, they are just typical instances of any alleged mutilation.

As more of these stories surfaced, the explanations seemed to get a little fuzzier as to what was going on throughout the Great Plains. Theories ranged from alien crafts gathering biological information from livestock for research, to pharmaceutical companies and the United States government testing agents and antibodies on living livestock, with chemicals taking a few weeks to take effect, and then biopsied to test the results. With the help of the media, suddenly everyone was a suspect. There were also several accounts of cult activity, in specific locations, gathering needed parts for ritualistic uses. In those cases, however, the causes of death were readily available and there were evident signs of struggle.

There was another interesting event that was told to me by a rancher in western Nebraska. He kept one of his bulls in a paddock near to his barn because he was a bit more ornery than the others, and they needed a break from him for a while. Early one morning, the rancher noticed his ornery bull staggering and walking like a zombie, and suddenly just fell over dead right in front of him. A veterinarian examined the bull and found a small, intravenous incision. The animal had been drained of almost all of his blood. The rancher mentioned that he wouldn't even approach the bull on some days because of his nature. He had no idea how anyone could have gotten to this animal, drained his blood, and then just walked away without being bulldozed by this massive and aggressive animal. Once again, no obvious evidence of an intrusion or struggle was ever found.

After digging into the written reports of these events, a pattern starts to emerge and always seems to lead to the more sinister types of explanations. There are those who are completely convinced that visitors from another world commit the crimes, and I must admit that some of their arguments can be convincing if you allow yourself to explore the possibilities. Hundreds of these reports are accompanied by the admission of several people who suddenly remember unusual aircraft in the area that mutilations occurred.

One of the most well-documented cases of this is of a craft that was visually located and followed by several law enforcement officers near Lebanon, Illinois, in the beginning of January 2000. Through the dispatch system several officers were able to follow the craft through multiple towns, and they now have collaborating stories for one incident. Reports can be found that further investigate and explain this incident on multiple webpages.

My conclusions are not any better than anyone else's. I feel more confused and misinformed when I study the subject, but numbers don't lie. Hundreds of reported mutilations are found to be the result of natural death and natural predators. Large numbers over the years have also been related to cult activity. That leaves the rest to be determined. Hundreds of cases have no definitive cause of death and to not have enough evidence to link the killings and mutilations to an obvious source. And these are only the cases that have been reported. There are a huge number of ranchers and farmers who don't even report the mutilations and just bury their dead animals, not wanting to know the cause.

One thing I know for sure is that anybody who has ever tried to sneak up on a herd of cattle, especially when calves are present, is out of their mind. They are by no means the dumb and docile animals they are portrayed to be. They will run you down, and there will be nothing you can do about it. As for me, the jury is still out about what is responsible for these mutilations, but there is way too much mystery tied to this subject to rule out any hypothesis.

So if you ever find yourself driving across the vast Great Plains, be sure to keep one eye on the sky. You just may find the answer to a mystery that is more than seventy years old. Just try not to become a part of it.

A Most Disturbing Curse

There is what some might consider a curse on the eastern plains of Colorado. It is so burdened with residual energy of an indescribable series of events, that some cannot even set foot on the ground without feeling or seeing what should be impossible.

History portrays Major John M. Chivington, aka the "Fighting Parson," as a bloodthirsty killer of Indians, a baby killer, and a vicious animal destined to exterminate all of the native peoples of Colorado. He was, at one time, regarded as a Civil War hero for saving the Colorado gold fields from the Confederates with two victories in New Mexico. He was also a clever man of battle, a minister, and adored by the people of the Colorado territory who were so proud to have a man of his stature in service to them.

There are a number of books written about what happened in the days leading up to November 29, 1864, but even with all the information available, this day still holds more secrets, lies, and conflicting accounts than any other event in U.S. history. What really happened that day can only really be known by those that lived it.

In the frigid, early morning hours of November 29, 1864, Chivington's Colorado volunteers already surrounded the village of Black Kettle. Cannons were aimed to soften the resistance of the enemy before troops on horses moved in. Holding "no quarter" orders, directly from Colorado's Governor Evans, Chivington knew what his military goal was. It was to quell, once and for all, the bloody Indian uprising in Colorado, to end the siege of Denver by the Indians, and to free the Smoky Hill and Platte river routes from constant attacks. At this time, the people of Denver were trapped and starving because the Indians were cutting off the river routes from all supply chains into the area.

Success by Chivington would secure trade routes to the territory and, most of all, to avenge the murders of Colorado settlers, which included women and children. The most well-known of whom was the Hungate family, who were reportedly murdered and horribly mutilated by a band of Arapahoe and Cheyenne tribesmen. Their bodies were found by freighters who brought them to Denver where the bodies were put on display, enraging the population of the frontier town who demanded military retaliation.

The following seven hours of battle is shrouded in conflicting reports. Evidence proves there was fierce resistance from the Arapahoe, which conflicts with the more popular belief that the camp was unarmed and consisted of mostly women and children. It is reported that Chivington and his Colorado militia brutally killed hundreds of women and children, and took a considerable amount of confiscated materials that were crated and shipped back to Denver in the days following the battle. However, there are also reports of freight papers from lost wagon trains, bloody clothing from settlers, and fresh scalps from white victims that are not popularized by today's historic point of view, but gives some proof that the encampment at Sand Creek may not have been the quiet- and peace-loving band of natives that it is popularly portrayed to be. Once again, only those who were there that fateful November day really know what happened.

In the weeks and months that followed, accusations began to arise about Chivington's Colorado volunteers. There were stories of rape, mutilation, scalping, and intentional killing of children. Reports started to surface from people on both sides that were present at the battle. White traders who were camped with the Arapahoe and Cheyenne told of horrific atrocities committed by the Colorado volunteers, while opposing views remarked that the encampment was fully armed, entrenched and anticipating Chivington's arrival. They even stated that many women and children helped to fight and, at the least, reloaded weapons for the warriors in rifle pits.

In the examination of the settlement of the west and the lack of response from the government, it is easy to see total and complete incompetence and confusion on the highest levels. Reactive and violent responses were commonplace in Colorado on both sides. The natives were reacting to several broken treaties that they didn't understand with the white man, as well as mistreatment and unfair dealings with the whites regarding everything from trade to misrepresentation of land ownership.

The white settlers, especially in the Colorado territory, were having their attitudes and opinions of the Indians molded for them in the biased opinions of the press. The Denver *Daily Commonwealth* went so far as to call for the outright extermination of all natives during this time period, and followed the now seemingly constant reports of attacks on settlers by Indians in the months leading up to the Sand Creek battle. They reported almost 200 deaths of settlers in Nebraska, Kansas, and Colorado, which is unheard of now in the modified accounts of that time. How many Indian deaths occurred, however, is another story. Various tribes were very efficient at hiding their actual death tolls in battle, and Sand Creek was no exception.

To draw a complete and final conclusion of what really happened on that day in 1864 may be historically impossible now. There has been too much tampering done with the evidence to hide fault or to propagate a predetermined opinion in favor of one viewpoint or another. It is, however, not hard to see multiple victims in this case: The settlers who were brought west by distorted views of the press that misrepresented availability of land that was already allotted to the local tribes by a treaty in an attempt to populate a given area with white Christian settlers. Major Chivington took heat for following the orders of his superiors in the territory, and when reacting to his responsibilities thrust on him by his superiors, and enraged attitudes of the white population fueled by the atrocities committed against the settlers. He became the scapegoat to protect a much higher political power, in my opinion.

Then there are, of course, the Arapahoe, Kiowa, Cheyenne, Ute, and Lakota people. They were the ultimate losers in a horrific political game. Thrown around like pawns, and expected to understand every time the government decided to alter their treaties that ultimately weren't worth the paper they were signed on. They were looked at as a hindrance to proper society and like unwanted dogs. There was a curiosity to those in the east who didn't live with or near them, and were considered a menace to those who did. Contrary to historical reports, there were many signs of compassion among native tribes. The Cherokee and Nez Perce tribes stand out as at least two who tried, to their own demise, to work out an acceptable peace with the whites to the east. It is understandable that, in the days of the great Indian wars, both sides had to fight, but specifically the Indians who had nowhere to go. They were backed into the proverbial corner with nothing but lies and misguidance as a baseline in dealings with the government.

Perhaps this is why it appears that the people of Sand Creek may not necessarily be at rest. Reports started as early as one year after the incident by a group of buffalo hunters who immediately reported seeing the encampment that was not suppose to be in the area. Scouts were dispatched to the location, but found no evidence of a camp. I have spoken with many visitors who have come to the actual site of the massacre, which varies some from the memorial site, who have reported feeling actual physical sickness, while others have reported an overwhelming feeling of sorrow. Not only that, but there have also been reports of seeing a large Indian encampment at the site that is somewhat shrouded by fog or mist on a wet, cold November evening. Ranchers on horseback, and even some bird hunters, as recent as just last year have seen the Indian encampment. It is a most disturbing place of death and remorse.

I have traveled many times through this area for work, and I must admit, I feel them. The feeling is so powerful that I expect to physically see them with their tattered clothes and starving horses. At times, I would stop my truck and step outside to feel the wind carrying the faint scent of sage, in an attempt to counter the near feeling of panic, pain, and sorrow.

A recent Colorado senator, who belongs to the Cheyenne tribe, claimed to have actually heard children crying at the site of the massacre; but his is not the only recollection of this disturbing occurrence among his people. Several members of the Cheyenne tribe have recalled hearing the sounds of death wails, and children crying in the early morning hours in November. The Sand Creek location was a reservation site chosen and agreed upon in a treaty for the Arapahoe and Cheyenne people. It was a very poor location with minimal food supplies.

The lost, lonely, and mournful feeling that some people get while driving across the plains is very real and has very real roots. It could quite possibly be a curse from years ago. It is a curse with a lesson that we must correct as best as we can. The problems of the past can be a lesson to all groups.

chapter four

The Supernatural Art of Scaring Outdoor Enthusiasts

You have worked all year for that one special vacation for you and your family; that one special time when your life is just spent seeking fun and surprises. You find that special campsite, the weather is perfect, and then that thing behind the tree on the path to the outhouse has to ruin it all. Your nine-year-old indicates that whatever it is has six eyes and eats toilet paper, and he will in no way attempt to go to the outhouse without you.

It seems the things we see on vacation are embedded into our memory banks and recorded in a different manner to be easily recalled the rest of our lives to bring a little smile to our face. From ghost trains to pony express riders who seem to go about their daily work, oblivious that their routes go right through the center of your campground, almost every state has vacation spots reported as being haunted. I have been told a few of these stories. Seriously, is the camping trip complete without a good ghost story?

The Pony Express

Interstate 80 through Nebraska traverses some of the most historic locations that were essential to the settling of the West. Unfortunately, many just pass it all by on their way to more publicized locations. Something unexplainable happens when you officially enter the west, crossing the Missouri River from Iowa and into Nebraska. The land changes somehow within the first fifty miles as you move west along the river that saw Indian tribes, canoes full of French trappers, and the Lewis and Clark expedition pass by the heavily wooded ramparts, witnessing the conversion of a fast moving, wild untamed river to a major commercial artery. Beginning at Lincoln and traveling west, you pass exits and draw ever closer to the Transcontinental Railroad Line, which seems to merge with I–80 at one point, and they stay within a stone's throw of each other seemingly all the way to the Pacific Ocean.

There are, however, much older roads right under the pavement in some places. The Oregon Trail followed the Blue River out of Kansas and stayed mainly to the south of the Platte River. The Mormon Immigrant Trail came from Iowa and eventually stayed primarily on the north of the same river to avoid conflict with travelers who did not approve of their religious beliefs and practices. North and south routes used to access strategically located frontier forts, cattle ranches, and new farming settlements intersected the Platte River Road, as it was formally called. Lastly, there was a route used for a little more than eighteen months by a business endeavor originating in St. Joseph, Missouri, for the sole purpose of finally linking the east with the west providing timely mail service.

The Pony Express was a bold enterprise spanning more than 2,000 miles, with 165 stations along the way. They hired only the best riders, with the average age being just eighteen years old. The youngest was only eleven and the oldest was in his mid-forties. They rode in all weather conditions, changed horses every ten to fifteen miles, and swapped riders around every seventy-five to one hundred miles, holding an average speed of ten miles per hour all the while. Thinking of the locations the Pony Express route traversed, one can only imagine what adversity those men must have endured, especially considering they rode through the heart of hostile Indian country unescorted, at full gallop, holding their light bodies close to their ride to maximize their speed.

The completion of a transcontinental telegraph system halted the Pony Express nearly as fast as it had begun, and riders were forced to move on to other careers. Some even became quite famous. Buffalo Bill Cody is one such man who moved on to becoming a western icon, whose love for the area has become an eternal landmark atop Lookout Mountain in Colorado, which is where he chose to be his final resting place overlooking the prairies he loved.

The Pony Express started in April of 1860, and officially ended in October of 1861. But if you talk to the right people, it would appear that some of the riders still seem to be employed by the Central Overland and California Express Company. In the Gothenburg area of Nebraska, it may be possible that a campground or rest area may have been built right in the middle of the central route. However, it doesn't appear that the new construction is in any way interfering with the timely delivery of letters and telegrams.

The westbound rest area along Interstate 80 near Brady, Nebraska seems to be one of those locations. It is a pleasant location with lots of trees and a nice facility far enough off the highway to make it comfortable. Unless, of course, you are walking your dog at about 2 o'clock in the morning. A truck driver was out with his dog when, in the distance, he heard the distinct sound of a galloping horse coming straight at him. As he grabbed his dog and jumped for the nearest tree, a horse and rider blasted by directly over the spot he and his dog were just standing. A cool rush of air followed the apparition, dressed in full western garb with the brim of his hat standing straight up in the front because of the high-speed rate of travel. The truck driver lost sight of the rider behind a camper blocking his view.

Other travelers have claimed to see a rider on the north side of the Interstate in the early morning hours. This rider seems to be what one would picture as a classic Pony Express rider. It is a very small-framed young man on a very fast horse with pouches on his saddle, and he always seems to be heading west. These riders are always going west, heading for the land that's fresh and new. Where hard working young men had a chance to dream, and to become what he wanted to be.

If your vacation plans ever take you through Nebraska, make sure to stop at one of the many museums that are within a stone's throw of Interstate 80. There is one that is actually built right over the highway. It will enhance your travels in more ways than can be counted. For a true lover of the west, it would be hard to fully understand and enjoy the area without experiencing in some way what the early immigrants encountered in their voyages.

They are all still there, waiting to be rediscovered by a family on vacation, and if you camp in the right location or find the right road at the right time, some of these characters straight out of the old west may just appear to be doing what they do best. Teaching their lessons to another traveler at some lonely wayside area.

The Ghosts of Register Cliff

The first, and most notable, identifiable landmark along the Oregon Trail is the Register Cliff in Wyoming. This site was used to assure travelers on the trail that they were on track for the easiest and most direct route over the continental divide, the South Pass. The tall sandstone cliffs were the perfect place to set up camp, meet others also migrating west, and scratch their names into the soft formation. Others that followed later could tell if someone they were concerned about had already been there. Hundreds of settlers signed the cliff, and it really is a must-see location for those interested in western and American history. Today it is an important piece of history. It is estimated that more than 500,000 settlers passed by this location between 1843 and 1869. Unfortunately, figures state that roughly 10 percent of these settlers died while en route; with their graves long since forgotten along the trail that even today passes through some very isolated areas. It was common for family members to pass away on the trail, and it seemed that if one member of the family succumbed to a fever, eventually the rest of the family would get it and perish one by one. Sadly, entire families died in this way, but very few died at the hands of Indians. More than the historical references, there are some well-known stories among the locals who live along portions of the old trail that suggest some ghosts are still present in the area.

One story in particular is of a weeping woman. She is crouched beside the trail between Register Cliff and Fort Laramie. It is believed she is mourning the death of a child lost during the great migration. She is dressed in the prairie dress common to that era with her face buried in her hands, sobbing.

Another well-known apparition roams the area as well, but has a different story. The agent in charge of Fort John when it was a trading post during the days of the American Fur Company had a daughter. She was visiting the trading post, but had asked to stay on a little longer so that she could spend more time with her father. She had the reputation of an accomplished horse rider and spent many days riding her horse across the prairies, while being escorted by men assigned by her father to keep an eye on her and protect her.

One day she decided to slip out and ride alone heading east of Fort John. Men tried to chase her and get her to stop, but that was the last time she and her horse were seen alive. Her father searched for days across the vast lonely prairies with no results. Eventually, he gave up the search for his beloved daughter and lived out the remainder of his life blaming himself for her death. It is believed that today his daughter can, indeed, be seen riding her stallion on the Oregon Trail east of the fort, wearing her green riding dress.

Fort Laramie, formerly Fort John, is itself also believed to be haunted. Park rangers and guests have reported footsteps near the cavalry barracks. Doors frequently open and close on their own, and lights have been seen inside buildings at night. This might not seem so strange, except these buildings are closed and have no electricity. Fort Laramie and the surrounding areas are steeped in history and indeed very haunted.

Disport Into the Past

The Yankee Hill Road is an increasingly more difficult primitive road that travels between St. Mary's Glacier and Central City in Colorado. These days, during the summer months it is a very busy place for people from the Front Range to bring their ATVs and beat the summer heat and enjoy a day in the mountains. Forest Service (FS) Road 175 and its adjoining trails are actually a trip back in time.

In the 1800s, it was regularly used as a stagecoach route as well as a transport route from mines in the area to the mills of Idaho. The road travels through the towns of Alice, Ninety

Four, Yankee, Cumberland Gulch, Pecks Flat, and the areas of Pisgah Lake, Bald Mountain, and Kings Flat, until finally terminating above Central City at the cemeteries. Several adjoining roads lead to other areas just as colorful. The list of towns sound like a railroad timetable, and coincidentally, some of these areas were on a railroad route beginning in the late 1800s, serviced by a little-known railroad called the Gilpin Tram (GT) powered by little steam-powered locomotives that fought incredible grades, tight corners, and impossible weather conditions. Much of the grades of this little railroad are still visible on the hills surrounding Central City and Blackhawk, as well as Russell Gulch.

The elevations slope gradually to the east, and at points you would think you could see all the way to Kansas and Nebraska. There are little valleys with cattle grazing on the deep grass, and cute little creeks and streams gurgling their way down the mountains and into the Platte system. The quaking aspens shimmering in the spring, lush green in the summer, and flickering gold in the fall mixed in with the dark-green lodgepole pine and Engelmann spruce. The rich smell of decaying vegetation mixed with the pines and the very pungent smell of the groves of aspen excite the senses; it is an olfactory experience that can reawaken hundreds of memories. For me it is very close to heaven, but there are some stories that would suggest that, for some, it might actually be heaven, or at least a good place to haunt until their departure to an even better place.

It seems the Gilpin Tram never really quit servicing the area, or there is audible evidence to indicate that there is at least one operating steam locomotive in the area. The shrill of a lone steam whistle has been heard as far west as Ninety Four at all hours of the day, but people have also heard them just over Winnebago Hill above Central City, mostly at night and sounding as if the little engine was pulling its train up and out of Chase Gulch. At this time there has been no sight of the train itself, but strange, dim lights have been seen following the old GT grade nearby, and on Quartz Hill trudging and plodding its way around the difficult grade south of Nevadaville, Colorado. The sightings of lights have definitely decreased in the past decade, mainly because access to the area is much more limited than it was until the late 1990s. But occasionally, a visitor will ask what it was they possibly could have seen in the wee hours of the morning while camping in the vicinity. My guess is that if it is possible for a piece of iron to leave some form of residual energy, it would have to beG3T; with her she took at least two mortal souls on to their reward, as she seemed to have much difficulty in minding her business and staying on the tracks. Her most memorable of wrecks was in Prosser Gulch on the bridge with new engineer Harvey Pierce at the throttle, G3T derailed and rolled over, crushing engineer Pierce to death and seriously injuring the fireman. Of course, she was rebuilt and put back into service, but a great deal of superstition exists in old railroaders, and for sure she was a marked and notorious engine until she was scrapped in the late 1930s.

A young family living in Colorado built an outdoor model based on the Gilpin Tram using scale equipment that was popular for outdoor garden railroad use. Upon its maiden voyage, with their nine-year-old son at the throttle, their steam engine eased onto their high bridge while Mom, Dad, and Baby Sister watched with grins on their faces. It was a perfect fall day as their summer project was coming to a climax, while their son blew the whistle and crept onto the thirteen-foot-high bridge that included two gondolas, one of which was carrying a video camera to capture the moment of the "little Gilpin's" maiden voyage. As the last car cleared the bridge, their son whistled twice to signify the all-clear and moving forward, and at that precise moment, very loudly and very clearly, was the unmistakable sound of a steam whistle far off to the east. Two short blasts signaling the all-clear and moving forward.

Many people in the area heard the whistle that fall afternoon, with no explanation as to where it may have come from. Unless of course it was old G3T, tipping her hat as if in thanks for keeping the memory of her existence alive. The family has long since moved, but it seems that the new owners of the house don't have the heart to tear the little Gilpin down. The high bridge still stands, totally visible to passersby, looking dilapidated and weathered. Her grade is still visible, just like the two-footer just over the hill to the east, fading into history with so few able to tell the real story about either of them as they drift off onto the dusty pages of the past.

This is not the only story originating from this area. An old schoolhouse still stands in what remains of the cute little town of Alice, Colorado. It was and, for the most part still is, the social centerpiece of this mountain community. Today it is used for large family gatherings, community events, and board meetings. The schoolhouse is well maintained and houses a wonderful little museum displaying local history and artifacts. The curator is always a very enthusiastic tour guide full of good recommendations regarding sightseeing. She can even give advice on hiking the glacier in the area, as well as its current conditions.

In the mid-1990s a family had a reunion at a residence only a few houses away from the schoolhouse. In those days the school was rarely used for anything other than meetings or a rare event, and it looked very forlorn. It didn't take long for the children at the reunion to realize that there was playground equipment in the old schoolyard, and they asked for permission to go to the schoolhouse and play. Permission was granted and the little kiddies ran off.

That evening at the family cookout, one of the adults asked if they had fun at the schoolhouse. One of the children replied, "Yeah, but tomorrow I wish we could play inside with the other kids on the real swing." The child's mother asked him to explain and he told her there were kids playing inside on better swings, but the doors were locked so they couldn't get in to see if they could play, too.

The mother's family had owned a cabin in the area for a few years but had never heard of swings inside the schoolhouse, so she wrote it off as the active imagination of her young son. Later that summer, over Labor Day weekend, the family returned to enjoy the cabin one more time before winter. While taking a walk, the same mother and son found themselves in front of the schoolhouse, but this time the doors were open. Inside was a woman sweeping the floors and tidying up the little place. The mother and her son walked up to the schoolhouse and asked if it was okay if they looked inside. She was excited to finally see the inside of the old one-room school, which still had its old chalkboard and a piano, but there were no swings.

She mentioned to the woman the funny request her son had made earlier in the year. At that moment her son exclaimed, "Momma they were right there!" He was pointing up to the ceiling at a steel bar that ran across the width of the room.

The woman explained to the mother that there were once swings there, but they had been gone for several decades. "Gosh. It may have been since the 1940s."

The swings attached to the steel bar so the kids could swing in the winter during their break when the snow got too deep for them to play outside. The child insisted that he saw kids playing in the room, and described a little girl who came to the window to look at him. She was wearing a pink dress and had curly brown hair. His mom thought it was very odd that her little boy knew so much of this. He had only visited the area a couple times, and was usually within earshot of his mother.

She looked down at her cute little son and said, "Honey, I believe you."

This schoolhouse is an absolute jewel and is being preserved by a dedicated group of people. There are not many one-room schoolhouses around, especially one that may still have regular students from another time.

History indicates the possibility of a curse on this little valley, originating from the Ute Indian tribe. The valley of the Fall River and its tributaries were sacred to the tribe and were sources of abundant game and pure water. The curse is said to be on the little valley to ensure that no white man would ever prosper there after it had been taken from the Utes.

A sacred burial site exists in the area, but the exact location is intentionally kept secret by a local resident who wants to keep people out of it. "There is no sense asking for trouble," he exclaimed when talking about its existence.

The earliest mining claim in the area dates back to 1860 and, most if not all, of the mining was unproductive. The location is near the border of rich silver deposits to the south and west, and rich gold deposits immediately to the east. The curse may have had some effect on its vacationers, as well, because the area has definitely had its share of freak accidents, missing persons, and fatalities—all mostly related to the area's recreational activities, the geographical severity of the area, and inexperience in the chosen activity. One fisherman cut his own leg off on a fall day in 1993 when it became stuck in the rocks at the edge of a lake. He crawled back to his truck and drove more than two miles on a rough trail to get to the first occupied house he could find to call for help. Fire personnel rushed to the lake to try and save the appendage and readily pulled his severed leg right out of the water. Was it possibly just a case of panic?

During the winter months the area is even more unforgiving. St. Mary's Glacier usually has very heavy snowfall and extreme wind conditions, which leads to heavy snow loading and avalanches. These severe conditions have led to a notable fatality rate, especially at the slide area east of the glacier. People navigating the top of the cliffs don't realize that they are actually walking on an eave of snow about twenty feet off the edge of the cliff. Many have accidentally made the trek without incident, while an unlucky few have not. I am told on windy winter nights, on the trails above the cliffs, those hardy enough for winter hiking and camping have told of hearing wolves howling to the north. The eerie sound is seemingly carried by the wind, and with the low moaning of the wolves, there is a cry for help, coming from the west or the north. It is impossible to tell, but it is out there somewhere in the horrific winds of January. Could it be a lost miner, hiker, or camper trapped forever in the curse of St. Mary's Glacier?

For those who camp in the area, and those lucky enough to do it in the off-season or during the week when there is very little traffic, seem to occasionally get a special treat outside their tents in the early morning hours. Those brave enough to admit it have heard mule teams and wagons passing by, their drovers barking at the mules. It seems to occur during the foggy evenings of late fall, along with sounds of a stamp mill operating down the hill, a faint hammering sound of an industry long since gone. On nights so foggy that you couldn't see ten feet in front of you if the sun was up—nights when you don't get too far from the tent when nature calls for fear you won't find your way back—it's a road that very possibly leads you to another plane or another reality as if there really are parallel worlds. And every now and then, the door opens and the fortunate few who have experienced it have seen the mines, the people, and the machines of an era of change and growth, an era of tragedy and triumph, an era that seems to refuse to completely disappear and will not let some of us forget what they experienced and why; from mine accidents to children who succumbed to one of many illnesses common at the time.

The area attracts those who are sensitive to the paranormal; be they visitors from far away or regulars who visit quite frequently, with no real reason why they have no interest at all in going anywhere else. To a night hiker or off-roader who, off in the distance, hear children playing in the vicinity of Pisgah Lake, it becomes a very real experience; a somber feeling overcomes them as they push toward York Gulch and evidence they are indeed still in the twenty-first century.

There's Something in the Woods

The Pike National Forest in Colorado seems to be centered in some of the state's vacation and recreational hot spots. It sits just west of Colorado Springs, surrounded by mountains and trails for visitors to explore the area. There are campgrounds that have been run by the families for decades. However, the area hasn't always been a recreational wonderland.

The Ute and Arapaho Indian tribes fought countless battles within the boundaries of what is now the National Forest. They were constantly fighting for territory and hunting grounds. They may have been fighting for something as simple as where they could gather supplies to live on. Not only did fierce battles take place on this land, but throughout the past several hundred years, countless lives have been lost in this area. Indians, miners, lost hikers, and even plane crashes have occurred there.

There is one specific hiking trail near the base of Pikes Peak that just doesn't feel right to visitors. There are feelings of cold on hot days, and it is not uncommon to hear of visitors panicking on this trail. Not only these feelings, but also many campers in the area over several years have reported seeing a wispy figure on the trails and in the campgrounds. The figure has been seen standing in the middle of trails, apparently trying to impede further travel. But most frequently, campers have seen him at night by the light of their campfires. He always stands at the edge of the firelight, just staring at the campers as if the campers amuse him. Although there is no way to prove it, it has been suggested that he may be the ghost of an old highwayman who was murdered more than one hundred years ago in the area of Little Fountain Creek.

Stories abound of this angry spirit attacking tourists and freighters in the late 1800s. The attacks were described as musty and nauseating, like being attacked by a rotting corpse. Could it be that, over time, the highwayman has mellowed a bit, fading into an echo of what he once was, and is now just a dark cloud or dark mist of energy roaming aimlessly through the forest? We may never know, but anyone in the area should be aware of something trying to spoil their fun.

Late-Night Fishing Fun

A friend once told me a story many years ago about a special fishing trip to Lake Marie in Missouri in the mid-1970s. For a late summer break, he decided to take his three sons to the lake for some night fishing while his daughters and wife stayed in the camper. It wasn't the best night for fishing, but the weather was very calm and the temperature was perfect, so he and his sons wanted to take advantage of that. After a few hours without any luck, the sons were still determined to catch fish, and their dad was comfortable to just sit back, relax, and enjoy the impeccable weather.

It was getting late into the night when my friend heard what sounded like a galloping horse racing directly toward them. Startled, he asked his sons if they heard it too, and they did. They said it sounded like the animal was going to run them down as the pounding hoofs were getting close, but it was so dark that they couldn't see anything. Just then, they all heard a loud splash indicating that the horse must have jumped into the lake. My friend scrambled to turn on his flashlight and shined in into the water where the noise came from.

There was not a single ripple in the water. He folded his chair and told the boys it was time to go back to the camper. He no longer wanted to sit in the dark near that lake, not knowing what it was that he just experienced with his sons. This story is still told in their family and is just as much a mystery today as it was on the night it happened.

chapter five

One Haunted
Little Town

The locals in an area near Central City, Colorado, all share a common belief. They all believe they are living side by side with ghosts. Many even go as far as admitting that their ghosts even try to influence decisions in the day-to-day life of those living in this mountain town. This is a thought that some paranormal investigators share, and it is backed up by hundreds of spirit communications. Of course, I also find myself drawn to this area.

In the late fall of 2012, I spoke to several people regarding the ghosts of Central City. The responses were much more than I should have gotten. Taking into account the population is just over 600 people, the amount of stories I got compared to the living people who reside there, Central City is one very haunted little town. Several years ago I was speaking to an elderly woman about the rumors of numerous hauntings in the town. She was shocked that I even needed to ask.

"Can't you feel them?" she exclaimed. "They are involved in everything we do."

A Gift from Yesterday

On a fall day in 2012, my wife and I were going to Central City to meet LeeAnna Jonas, who was the proprietor of the Spirit Realm Investigative Project (SRIP). Amazingly, she had set up a group of interviews for me to gather information for this book. My daughter, who was sixteen years old by this time, wanted to come with us, but LeeAnna suggested she stay away from the location for the first interview because the residence had a particularly disagreeable vapor. She thought that my daughter could be in danger because younger people can be more sensitive to these things. Although she was disappointed, my daughter understood and decided to go shopping at the gift shop on Main Street. It was really more of a gift shop and antique shop rolled into one.

My daughter got lost in all of the things the store had for sale. She found a music box that played a song from her favorite movie and she just had to have it. While going through her purse, she found that she would be a few dollars short of the twenty-dollar asking price. Saddened, she put her money back in her purse, looked at the music box one last time, and started to walk away. As she was walking she heard a voice behind her.

"That's really cute isn't it?" a woman said. She was an older woman, wearing clothing that was popular during the

Victorian period. My daughter agreed with her and told the woman why she loved it, and also why she wasn't able to buy it.

"I will give you ten dollars for it," the older woman said.

Confused, my daughter replied, "Oh, I don't own it."

"No, no," the lady said. "I will give you ten dollars so you can buy it. You have the other half, correct?"

Excited, my daughter replied, "Are you serious?"

The woman nodded her head and had a grin on her face as she gave my daughter the money. To that, my daughter gave her a big hug and thanked her repeatedly. The woman's name was Mary Ann and they chatted a bit. My daughter thanked her again and shook her hand. My daughter turned around to pick up the music box and when she turned back, Mary Ann was gone.

She was nowhere to be seen. My daughter even checked both levels of the store. Mary Ann seemed very real, but an exit like that would have been impossible. It is not uncommon to see people dress in period clothing during this time of year in Central City.

Haunted Coffee

Jeanne Bower was the owner of a coffee shop in Central City who had to come to an uneasy understanding with her ghost. It seemed that whatever was at her business was not of the friendly variety. She experienced constant, unexplainable issues with her refrigeration equipment that ended up costing her hundreds of dollars in spoiled food. Then, the entity started tampering with other appliances. Coffee makers were turned on and burning up when the shop was closed, but thankfully it never got to the point of causing a fire.

Not only did she have problems in her business, but Jeanne also had issues on all three floors of the building that she was leasing. Lightbulbs were repeatedly unscrewed in the stairwells, where it was unsafe enough for lights to be required. Voices were audible in the building, including a crying baby, that has been heard by multiple people at all hours. A curtain that separates a food storage area from the bar area in the coffee shop opens and closes as if someone is walking through it as well.

In multiple investigations by the SRIP team, the name Grant kept coming through. There were other names as well, but it appeared that Grant was the feisty one causing all of the trouble. It seemed that this ghost would continue to be a problem for the business. It got to the point that I wanted to go upstairs and have a talk with her ghosts to see if I could demand that they stop bothering her, but the experts advised that I just leave them alone.

The SRIP team believed that this Grant was of an evil nature and was not to be fooled with, especially by amateurs. The team was made up of all females, and one of the crew members was repeatedly being touched in an aggressive and sexual manner. It was so bad that she had to stop working at this location. Not only that, Jeanne had a hard time keeping employees at the shop for more than a couple of weeks.

Unfortunately, the coffee shop has since closed because Grant wasn't very willing to share the space with Jeanne and her customers. We will have to see if another business wants to try their hand in this spot, and take on Grant and his ghosts.

Mountains of Ghosts

"DON'T MESS WITH MY GHOSTS!" Sandy, an employee at the Mountain Menagerie gift shop in Central City, exclaims. She seems to have a good working relationship with the ghosts that roam her workplace. She has worked there for more than seven years, and has seen her fair share of paranormal activities during that time.

Things really began to pick up when a wall was removed between the gift shop and the candy shop next door. There are stories of hearing furniture being moved in the upper levels where there is no furniture, clothing racks and items on shelves being rearranged nightly, the sound of children rolling a ball across the floor, a chair sliding across the upstairs floor, and shoppers claiming they heard voices while walking through the front door or by the restrooms. The sounds of kids singing and playing are heard on a regular basis, especially from the candy shop and from the upstairs levels. Sandy, and several others, also regularly heard balls rolling across the floor, and music boxes playing. A child singing a lullaby could frequently be heard at the candy shop, and was apparently the cause for high employee turnover.

One night at closing time, four music boxes and a Christmas clock playing a carol all went off at once, which had never happened before. Three of the music boxes were found at the opening to the candy shop, which was several feet from where they were displayed on a shelf in the main part of the gift shop.

A woman was startled by a little girl standing at the top of the stairs while walking to the upper floor of the store. The woman gasped as if she was startled, and the ghost girl gasped and said, "I am sorry for scaring you."

Some of this activity has been recorded on security cameras that were installed after a water main broke on the block. During the water main problem, a firefighter confided in me that while he was inspecting the buildings for damages and safety issues, he kept hearing a voice behind him. He even felt someone tapping him on the back, which takes a pretty hard tap in all the gear he was wearing.

Sandy said it is not uncommon for a visitor to walk in the door and abruptly turn right around and leave, refusing to come back with their family. She said it seems like some people catch on pretty quickly that the place is haunted, while others think it's fun. Sandy also feels a strong connection to this town, even though she's not a native. She intends to stay right there because the pull this little town has is just too strong for her.

A Ghosty on Your Neck

Josie came to Central City in 1981 as a drummer and later became a local concert promoter. He and his wife also own one of those old-time photo shops in town that took pictures of my wife and me in a cowboy and barroom floozy costume on our honeymoon in 1987. You can decide who wore which costume ...

Josie had a love for the area, but admitted it took quite some time before he felt accepted by many of the locals. Oddly enough, it was kind of a mini magnet for musicians. There was even an especially famous recording studio nearby with some very famous rock musicians being seen and heard in those days. It didn't take very long before Josie found himself wrapped up in his first paranormal event.

He was innocently walking around the town enjoying his time off as a road musician. He happened to meet a frail elderly woman on the steps of the courthouse. They instantly began talking about the town and its features. The banter quickly turned from architecture and festivals to a dark, secret confession that Josie vividly remembers to this day.

The woman brought up a story about her father and the lost courthouse gold. Apparently, her father had worked at an assay office in Central City with one of his good friends. There happened to be a robbery at the office that the owner wanted to keep quiet so not to cause panic over the lost gold. The owner managed to keep the robbery a secret but fired all of the employees, including this woman's father, because he was certain that the crime was an inside job. Her father and his friend eventually found another job that put them on a crew building the new courthouse in 1889.

On his deathbed many years later, the woman's father admitted that it was he and his friend who indeed did steal the gold from the assay office. In his confession, he said that they decided to hide the evidence by building it into the walls in the basement of the new courthouse, which they were able to do. While in the process of doing this, however, he admitted that the men got in to a heated argument over the loot, and he killed his friend.

With great remorse days before his death, the woman's father said, "I killed my best friend and buried him with the gold in one of the basement walls of the courthouse." Even worse than that, he also confessed that after he sealed up the wall, he started to hear scratching from inside the wall. His friend wasn't completely dead. He realized he had buried his friend alive.

Understandably, Josie started to have an uneasy feeling as the conversation progressed, and he tried to politely cut the exchange short and walk way. He tentatively took a few steps away from her and turned around to look back at her, but she was gone. There was no way this frail, elderly woman could have moved as fast as it would have taken to be out of site in the two seconds it took him to take a few steps and look back.

A few years later, Josie got a job with the county doing building maintenance. Being an employee, Josie had access to the county offices and buildings before and after regular working hours. This gave him the privilege of possible experiences with ghostly activity, as you would expect.

In 2011 the SRIP team was allowed to investigate the building after years of trying. Josie was chosen to be their guide because no one else knew the buildings as well as he did. He told one member of the team about the story he was told so many years before about the gold robbery, but for some reason she failed to tell the rest of the team before the investigation. Josie said the basement was a great place to talk to his co-workers or mumble to himself stuff like, "My job sucks. I am having all these women problems. Working here all these years to pay child support, can't get nowhere, etc."

The team began their investigation when LeeAnna started to hear a voice coming over her *ovilus*, which is a ghost box device that scans hundreds of frequencies, searching for voice phenomenon. The voice she was hearing was persistent and kept repeating the words "gold" and "trapped" while they were in the basement. Suddenly, her teammate revealed her conversation with Josie just hours before. Excited, LeeAnna wondered why her teammate hadn't said anything earlier and figured out that the repeated words now made sense.

LeeAnna spoke into the dark to whoever it was that was trying to communicate with her and said, "Josie told us about you. Do you know who Josie is?" Within a few seconds the ovilus put out a few more words:

"Marriage ... problems ... affair ..."

"Wow," LeeAnna said. "He's telling his story."

Shocked and surprised, Josie laughed and said, "No! He's telling *my* story!" knowing full well that this ghost was probably listening to him mumble about his problems in that basement.

While I was interviewing him, Josie laughed and said, "Holy shit man. I should have kept my mouth shut! It's like this close-knit community," he said. "You can't keep any secrets." Josie experienced other problems in the courthouse, as did other employees. It was just the usual stuff; doors opening and closing, paperwork being reorganized, and an occasional ghost sighting by more than one person.

One of the more memorable stories was when, after repeated problems with the courthouse's fire alarm, representatives from a well-known alarm company came to diagnose and repair the failing system. They discovered there was an issue between the annunciator in an upper level and the main control panel in the basement. Josie heard one of the men mutter to his colleague that what was going on with the system was physically impossible. After more diagnosis, one of the alarm techs began testing the sensors with a smoke tube on the lower floors where the sensors could not be easily reached. The roof was low enough on the third floor to not need the tube to test the equipment.

The tech leaned the tube against the wall and began to proceed down a hall to conduct the test. He heard what sounded like a tree branch rubbing hard against a glass window at the end of the hall, so he went to investigate what was going on. He found that there was not a tree, or anything else, that could rub against the glass. He turned around and started to walk back down the hall. He looked up just in time to see his smoke tube flying through the air, straight at his head. He ducked just in time and the tube narrowly missed him. He ran downstairs and told the other tech what had happened, and said that was the last time he would ever work in that building.

Surveillance cameras have picked up movement in just about every area of the building, but what seems to be the most active area is in the records vault and the old jail cells.

Moving chairs and paperwork floating around the office are common. Josie worked every other Saturday and an employee of the assessor's office saw his truck parked outside the building one weekend, but knowing the schedule, she didn't pay any attention when she heard furniture being moved on the floor above her. That is until she looked out the window and saw Josie on the sidewalk talking to a police officer. The employee quickly finished up what she was doing and decided to call it a day. Unlike some, she didn't quit her job because of these types of events. She just wasn't comfortable being alone in the building.

Josie did, however, have a real problem in the jail area of the building. This jail seems to be home to a number of ghosts, but there is one that seems to be particularly evil, and may have even attached itself to Josie. In 1995 Gilpin County built a new justice center. This upgrade was desperately needed because the jail in the courthouse building was very old and very primitive. Josie said that jailers would bring prisoners outside for some fresh air each day, and they looked pale and had to squint their eyes to transition from the dark and gloomy to sunny and bright.

Following the completion of the new justice center, the county moved the jail and sheriff's department to the new building, but because of a delay with the electronics equipment, the dispatchers remained in the basement of the courthouse. Almost immediately, the nighttime dispatchers started to hear footsteps on the first floor when the building was suppose to be empty and locked up tight. Being police dispatchers, deputies and local police officers all searched the building following these reports, but found nothing out of the ordinary. Except for some nervous dispatchers.

After the SRIP investigation of the building in 2011, many of the employees insisted that things began to get much more active. It got to the point that they didn't know if they wanted any more investigations to take place. One of the employees of the county assessor was leaving the restroom during her regular workday when she encountered a mother walking with her young daughter next to the entrance to the women's restroom. The little girl, who was probably three years old at the most, was pointing down the hallway with a distressed look on her face.

The young girl was yelling, "GHOST! GHOST!" The mother of the young girl tried to laugh it off and started apologizing to the employee and explaining that this was not typical behavior for her daughter. Not surprisingly, Josie confirmed a few days later that doors had been slamming, and window shades were torn from the wall in the area that the little girl had been looking and screaming.

There was soon attention from TV producers who were adamant about needing access to the courthouse for a show on hauntings. The SRIP team, along with Josie, did eventually do a piece for a TV program on the building. The location still seems to have issues even today. It's pretty hard to explain and rationalize flying objects, slamming doors, and moving phantom furniture. Pretty much everyone can agree with that.

Haunted History

The executive director of the Gilpin County Historical Society, David Forsyth, works exclusively in a haunted place. I did not have nearly enough time when I interviewed David. If I were to choose one person to give me a guided historical tour through Gilpin County, it would be him. Besides the fact that his sense of humor would have your sides hurting, you would learn a great deal about the area.

In September and October of each year, David helps organize the Creepy Crawl, which is strictly about ghosts, so it is a perfect haunted tour of the town. With locals are dressed in period costumes, telling original ghost stories at the exact locations that they occurred, this wonderful event is the perfect way to welcome the fall season. It is fun to see people walking the streets of Central City dressed in the fashions of the 1880s, and at times it feels like you are physically transported back in time to those days.

David begins his tour of the Creepy Crawl saying, "Welcome to Central City, Colorado. Where every building but one is haunted." The Thomas House appears to be the only house in the city that has no recorded events of paranormal activity. Thinking of the size of town and the events that have occurred in many of the buildings, this is a powerful statement. With this in mind, however, David insists that he has never felt threatened, but he has had to set things straight with some of his ghostly acquaintances.

One of his interactions was at a building called Washington Hall. Today it is the site of a small museum, but in 2008 it was an art gallery with a gift shop on the lower level. David was opening the building one morning and walked to the back room when he heard a very loud voice from behind him exclaim "We are closed!" David spun around and didn't see anything in the building. He walked back outside and looked up and down the sidewalk, thinking maybe someone was walking by talking on a cell phone, but there was nobody in sight. David turned around and went back into the building, announcing that the shop was most definitely open.

David works at the Gilpin County Museum where he organizes projects and gets things ready for the upcoming seasons. David was working alone on a tourism exhibit when he heard a female voice say, "Oh, he's in here." Understandably, David was startled. He jumped and spun around, and once again there was no one there. He initially thought that a member of the board was in the building, but after searching the premises he realized that he was the only person in the building. He thought about just going home that night, but refused to let this entity get the better of him.

About two weeks later, the motion detectors at the entry doors started to go off continuously, as if people were entering and leaving the building. Each time, David would poke his head out of his office to see who it was but found no one in the museum. It became more of a problem, and he once again searched the entire location and found no one.

He finally had enough so he marched up the steps and yelled down, "It's okay if you are in here, but when I am here by myself you need to please leave me alone." Things quieted down for about two or three weeks after that, but then the alarms gradually began to go off again on both levels of the museum.

This time David was agitated, and he angrily reasserted what he had said before. "Look, I told you it was okay to be in here, but I asked you that when I am in here alone you are to leave me alone. AND I MEANT IT!"

David hasn't had any trouble since he put his foot down, but he knows the ghosts are still there with him. He accepts that and seems to have a good working relationship with them.

When he mentioned these incidents with a co-worker and board member, they matter-of-factly replied, "Oh, yes. She's a female and is normally upstairs." They also thought that she was happy that they were taking care of the building. As if David needed more confirmation, a daughter of a board member had worked as a guide at the museum. She informed her mother that she was convinced the museum was haunted, and that it was a woman who seemed to favor the Victorian room, which was decorated in period furniture and accompaniments of the period. This room is the only place in the entire museum where David feels uncomfortable. This is mostly because a number of people have confirmed that they believe there was a regular ghost in that room.

Another event took place in the museum while David was giving a tour. He was asked by one of the guests if they could take pictures inside the building. David stated that it was fine as long as he was not in the picture, because he doesn't enjoy having pictures of himself taken. Within a few minutes, a number of the women began gathering around him and snapping pictures of him. He chuckled, thinking that they were just poking fun at him, but one of the photographers pointed out that orbs of light in fact surrounded him, and their digital cameras were capturing them. It was a general consensus that the ghosts apparently really like David.

David is full of historical information pertaining to this area. He knows the people, either living or long since passed, and is a living link to the past. He takes his responsibilities seriously and can tell visitors a great deal about the stories that help to give the town great color and character. At the end of my interview, David made an interesting observation that I strongly agree with. He noted that the ghosts of Central City seem to like him very much, and it is him that they have chosen to relay their messages.

He calmly stated, "If they expect me to be their messenger, then they are going to have to speak up."

To Die or Not To Die

It can be so hard to understand what the mindset of someone is when they have hit rock bottom, and when they feel they have nowhere to go and no friends or family to confide in. There always seems to be an attraction to the little mountain towns that hold a profound power over some people. Like everything, this attraction can have both good and bad sides to it. Repeatedly, people have come to these areas to end their lives. Possibly thinking that if they are going to die, why not do it in a beautiful place? I had the privilege of talking to a wonderful woman who came to the cemeteries above Central City to do just that. Strangely, however, it would seem that someone from the other side wasn't going to let her destroy her soul in that manner.

As she sat in the grassy meadow that cold evening near the cemeteries, something spoke to her in a seemingly telepathic way. She recalls that the words were as comforting as if they were coming from her own mother. Whatever or whoever was speaking to her talked her down from the desire to kill herself, and she began to weep uncontrollably as she realized that she wanted to live. She even confessed to repeated contact with this unknown entity after the incident and has since moved to the area. She has also become a devout Christian and now works right in Central City.

Sadly, others didn't fare so well. In 2011 a young man from Illinois decided to go to the Rockies and drive his car over the side of the mountain. Just in case the fall and sudden smash at the bottom didn't do the job, the man brought a gun with him as well. The young man somehow chose the wrong section of the road to veer off because the fall didn't end up killing him. Instead, he slid out of control down the steep hillside and came to a stop about 200 yards below the highway. While several witnesses were present at the scene, a gunshot was heard from the car while they were calling 9-1-1. Sadly, the young man died in a helicopter en route to Denver. A local mortuary made arrangements to have the young man cremated and have his remains brought back to his family in Denver. They were going to spread his ashes over the mountains that he so loved.

While transporting his remains over the same area where his car was thrown off the road, the transporting vehicle inexplicably pulled hard to the left and somehow removed itself from the roadway. The action ejected the driver out through the sunroof of the vehicle, leaving him a bit disoriented but completely unharmed. The vehicle, however, had managed to travel about 500 yards from the roadway into an aspen grove. A responding state patrol officer mentioned the accident to the tow truck driver on the scene. Coincidentally, they were both the same people who had responded to the suicide attempt just one week earlier.

"You remember that accident up here last week? The suicide?" the tow truck driver asked the office. "I still have the car in my yard."

"In that tree down there are the ashes of that young man, in perfect condition," the officer said.

I have seen both of the vehicles involved in this story, and there is no explanation as to how the driver of the transport vehicle could have been ejected and still survived with as badly as the van was torn up. The driver walked away from this horrific accident with only bruises from his seat belt. There was no evidence as to why the vehicle suddenly left the roadway. If you think about what the officer said about the man's ashes, it seems like maybe he wanted to be in one piece and be where he initially planned to die.

A Ghost Town Dies

The small towns of Blackhawk and Central City in Colorado have an incredible past. Their histories are truly the stories of the old American West. Their beginnings were much like all other gold and silver mining towns in the area at the time. There were beautiful valleys and streams, and underneath had rock infused with veins of silver and gold. Some of it was exposed because of billions of years of erosion, and then flowed perfectly into the creeks as if they were leading the inevitable searchers to their locations. It was like a natural treasure map that eventually made Colorado the perfect candidate for statehood. The prospectors, who were later called the 59ers, began their search by exploring Colorado ten years after the gold finds in California in 1849. The towns have only survived since then largely because of tourism.

In the late 1980s, an idea sprang up that had many of the locals convinced it was the end of their little towns. Gambling had made its debut in Colorado. In the fall of 1991, it was as if the two towns were holding their collective breaths on a decision that had already been made. Months before the decision went to the ballot boxes, property owners in both towns were made offers that they couldn't, and had better not, refuse. Others who weren't offered the payout lost their properties anyway to condemnation, only to find out that a national gambling chain had somehow acquired their property without correcting the issues that got it condemned in the first place.

The people of Central City and Blackhawk confirmed their loss before taking a vote. Many citizens took one last look at the place that their families had lived for generations and hoped that in some way the towns would be preserved. There were some residents, however, who weren't ready to give up the fight, and started to stage a battle of their own. I spoke with Bruce, a former Central City police officer, who had some incredible stories to tell from 1991 and 1992, and some even appear to be happening even today.

Almost immediately, the displeasure over how the two towns were treated became evident while Bruce and I were talking. Some of the buildings still contained original furnishings and hardware. When the changes came, these things were stripped completely, even removing the floors. The contents were then auctioned and carted away to all corners of the country. Once nightfall came, the officers noticed some strange things happening. Doors were opened and unlocked after officers had confirmed they had indeed been locked. Fire alarms were repeatedly set off in buildings that were being reconfigured, and then there were the intrusions.

Bruce got a call one night about a suspicious person in what he believed to be the Gilpin Hotel in Blackhawk. When he arrived at the hotel he found an open door, so he relayed this to his dispatcher and requested backup from the local sheriff as he entered the building. As he entered, Bruce identified himself and began to search the premises with only the light of his flashlight. He heard what sounded like heavy footsteps on the floor above him. Once again he announced who he was, and that the perpetrators should give themselves up. The sheriff's deputy had shown up, so Bruce decided to go up the stairs to check it out. While Bruce was upstairs, the deputy was going to watch the stairway and first floor.

By this time, a second Gilpin County car had arrived because both officers had heard the footsteps, confirming that someone was indeed on the property. Bruce began a door-to-door search with his weapon drawn because whoever was in that building was not responding to his requests. The three officers searched the entire building that night, and absolutely nothing and no one was found. They had no choice but to have a confused sense of humor about what at first had appeared to be a possibly dangerous situation.

Seemingly out of danger, the sheriff's deputy had other responsibilities and left Bruce as he climbed back into his patrol car parked in front of the hotel. He started to fill out his report on the incident and let his dispatch know that he was available for other calls. As he finished his report and put his clipboard on the passenger seat, he pulled his car out and glanced at the dark building one more time. This time he saw a face glaring down at him from a second-story window that appeared to be a young woman. She slowly faded away as if she was on a track moving her backward, and Bruce recalls that she was wearing Victorian clothing. An employee at a former hotel in Central City also stated that in the final days at the hotel, the beds were being turned down and water was being put into the washbasins on the floor that had no water and no guests staying.

Almost daily we would take people on tours of these floors to show them the history of the hotel and how it would have looked. One of the visitors mentioned that it was nice that the tour had made the room look as if it was ready for a guest to check in. I agreed, but knew that it wasn't the tour that had done that. On one occasion, we were getting ready to close for the day, so I was checking the halls to be sure that every one was gone and to lock up, when I saw a woman walk across the hall from one room to another. I screamed and ran downstairs. A couple of my co-workers went back up to see what or who was there, and found nothing. That is how my last days at the hotel were spent. I never really got used to it, but just began to accept it. It all started to make sense when one of my co-workers mentioned that within the next year the place would not be the same, and maybe those entities just aren't happy about it.

Even today, some of those buildings in their original conditions encounter unlocked doors, pulled breakers, open windows, and dozens of other occurrences where they shouldn't happen, and seems to be the result of unhappy inhabitants. Repeated contacts by paranormal investigators support the idea that indicate the spirits or entities are not at all happy with the changes that have been made to their homes.

The promised preservation of the towns was a lie. Central City was left untouched more than Blackhawk, which is almost unrecognizable. Complete mountains were removed; it is now the home to several high-rise buildings, as well as countless parking lots and commercial buildings. Those who were forced to move out of the towns all have the same feelings. More power to the ghosts.

September Shadows

The business of ghost hunting was all a mystery to me. I wanted to see how it worked and I wanted some answers, as if I needed any more proof after living in our own haunted house. But I needed more confirmation, more insight, and more understanding of what could possibly be happening. These questions led me to a local mine shaft that would hopefully help me find out what was going on and why I was experiencing these things. The evening of September 11, 2012, will forever be burned into my memory as the turning point in what could be considered spiritual consciousness. This was the classic evening for ghost hunting in Gilpin County, Colorado.

The drive from my house was dreary with heavy fog and drizzle dropping off the surrounding peaks. I discussed with my wife the benefit of taking a different route than we normally take because it was a good way to prepare my mind for what we were heading to do that night. In reality, it was a delay. It was an intended distraction to help me deal with the apprehension that was welling in my mind. I'm not sure if it could be called fear, but it definitely put into question my personal beliefs. Even though my experiences involving the paranormal prior to this night were numerous, they were based on suppositions and encounters that could not be explained by anyone with any expertise on the subject.

The Coeur D'Alene Mine is a forlorn place, and its past resembles the histories of most of the mines in the area. There were multiple owners, multiple failures, unimpressive production, and accidental deaths. It started in the 1880s, and was originally named the Academy Hill Mine. In early photographs, it appears that the mine was a well-kept operation.

It's not documented when the name was formally changed, and thankfully the mine was still in operation during World War II. This saved it from being dismantled in the scrap drives that eliminated many historical operations.

The mine was in horrible condition in the 1980s, and it looked as if those taking care of the property were going to just let it crumble; in the mid-1980s the building partially collapsed. A decade later, funding came from the Colorado Historical Society, the Colorado Lottery, and the gaming industry. The funds were used to repair the little mine on the hill and open it up as a museum. It stands today as an excellent example of what type of mining structures were used and were so common in the area long ago.

The mine sits perched precariously on a hill above Central City. A group of ghost hunters were there unloading their gear in anticipation of our arrival. As we approached the mine, I turned to my wife and daughter to ensure they were ready for what we were likely to encounter that night. What they didn't realize was that I was just thinking out loud, and really questioning myself as well to be sure that I was up for it. I was realizing that my entire life's journey might have always been drawing me to this situation. I needed the maturity that comes with living a difficult life, and possibly needed the discipline that only time can instill in your soul to be able to perform the task that had been placed on my shoulders. It seems that I had been brought here for some reason. Lured in by the history, the trains, and the surroundings, but for what purpose? As we entered through the sliding door of this old structure, I was overcome with feelings that almost brought me to tears. Despite that, I put a smile on my face and announced we had arrived.

As the door closed behind us, one of the girls said, "The fun now begins."

On this cold and wet September evening, the drizzle picked up to a steady rain that pounded on the roof of the mine. The mine has no electricity, so we had only half an hour for LeeAnna and the SRIP team to brief us on how that night's work would be conducted, and what we could expect to happen. After that, it was total darkness. For some reason, LeeAnna was very concerned about the possibilities of what could happen that night, so she asked that we all say a prayer together before we started. LeeAnna thought that my unexplainable interest in the area, the history, and that I wanted to write about the area was not a coincidence.

This mine itself holds a special interest to me. Just starting out in life after my wife and I got married in 1987, I was no different than any other twenty-one-year-old man at the time. We didn't have much extra income and I loved being home with my wife on the evenings and weekends, so my hobbies were all things that I could do at home. One of these happened to be building an exact scale model of the Coeur D'Alene Mine. I always had a love for Central City, and this mine was a kind of landmark for me. There was some sort of strange pull and I wanted to build a model to preserve this mine. It was a way to save the memory of this wonderful structure for me.

Up until that evening in 2012, I had never physically set foot in this building, but I knew exactly where everything was located. I knew the vertical shaft, the boilers, and the water tank would be exactly where I thought they would be. Here we were attending a real ghost investigation, and I was busy making comparisons to elevations I had studied some twenty-five years prior.

Armed with night-vision cameras and digital recorders, we began our investigation of the building. Feeling like nothing more than an observer, I began to move through the little building with LeeAnna and her team. The rain started to let up as LeeAnna introduced us to the spirits that she thought were there. One of the team mentioned that they had a new, somewhat primitive, tool that their friend had made for them to help detect spirits. After being briefed on the thousands of dollars' worth of technological equipment the team already had at their disposal, who made them, and what exactly they were suppose to detect, imagine my surprise to find out they were in fact divining rods! They were the same rods that my grandfather used years ago to find water as a young man.

I was thrilled! My grandfather was an expert within their use, and I learned what they were used for from him, so I became very good at them, too. I even used them in my job as a heavy equipment operator, and always seemed to do quite well against the guys who were using expensive equipment to find underground utilities. Oddly, the best set of rods I have ever used were the ones that I made out of a pair of coat hangers. They were so lightweight they enabled me to feel the slightest magnetic pull. You have to be able to feel the subtlest of reactions to the rods, so the lighter the rod, the more responsive they seem to be. The rods need to be able to move freely, and the set that the SRIP team had were made of heavy copper so I told the team that, in my opinion, they wouldn't work. Despite my opinion, we decided that with my background and experience, I would give them a try anyway.

Armed with the divining ods, I was now an integral part of the investigation operat g the experimental equipment. I moved around a bit to see if the rods would work and to see how they felt in my hands. Sadly, they performed exactly as I had predicted. They were very numb, and only the strongest pulls were detectable. I didn't feel a thing when I passed over a pipe, and when I passed over a vertical mine shaft I only felt a faint draw on the rods. They were too heavy, and I wished I had brought my homemade ones with me. Despite this, I decided to keep the rods with me and see what might happen as the night went on. I would be glad I did.

For the sake of the recordings, LeeAnna formally announced why we were there and that I was included in the investigation because of researching for this book. She spoke into the darkness, mentioned some contacts with spirits they had experienced in the past, and what her intentions were for this particular evening. Other than the team, the only movement in the mine was a little bat that fluttered around us a bit as we walked deeper into the structure. It would fly around our heads every once in awhile, but it finally found its way outside for the night.

As the night wore on, my fingers started to go numb as I held the rods as steady as I could. For a time, I became so wrapped up in watching the team doing their work that I forgot I was even holding them—until they moved. The communications came slowly, but there was no mistake that it was communication. The EMF meter, which measures electromagnetic fields, started spiking at some specific locations in the building. In a building with no electricity, I was perplexed as to what could possibly be causing these spikes.

LeeAnna started to ask questions out loud into the darkness to try and get some sort of response from any inhabitants. The first question she asked was for a sign to let us know they were there. The response came with the sound of a metal object banging against one of the boiler doors. Then, a brand-new battery that was just installed minutes before was completely drained in one of the instruments.

At exactly eighteen minutes and fifteen seconds into our recording, while the team was trying to figure out what was going on with the batteries, a female voice was recorded. She said a three-syllable word, but I am not even sure it was in English. It sounded more like and Irish or Gaelic term. Then shortly after that, movement could be visually detected in the hoist area, which is where the mine would bring things up from underground. In this area, the little light that was coming in through the window was being erratically blocked.

Once again, LeeAnna spoke into the darkness and stated, "This is your chance to have your story told. We have a writer here that is interested in you." She then started to ask more personal questions about the entity. Its name, occupation, and how they died. As she was asking them questions, we found several voices overlapping on the recorder in the room, and their voices were unintelligible.

We decided to move to another location closer to the boilers. Weak sounds and movements in the building were becoming more frequent. It was as if the first few spirits that we encountered went and got their friends and came back. After LeeAnna had a physical reaction feeling someone choking her and having difficulty breathing, we moved back to the center of the building. We took a break for a few minutes to collect our thoughts and decide how we should proceed for the rest of the evening.

Soon the ovilus started kicking out several words, indicating that there could be many more than just one contact with us, and was making it difficult to make any sense out of the words. The more LeeAnna communicated, the more definite the messages became. She had two names she was working with, one of which was a man named Paul. One message came through with what appeared to be a warning: Evil...Demon...Run...

After this grouping came through, the messages started coming through more frequently and more friendly. They even seemed to have some similarities to previous contacts that we had talked to. One even said the word "kiss." Realizing this meant it was time for us to go, it was suggested we move back to the central part of the building to take a break. Shortly after we moved to the new location and sat down, we started to experience visual, audible, and physical communication. Rain was again pounding the roof of the building as we all noticed movement under the water tank behind the boilers. Without a doubt, this was the darkest part of the room, and I noticed movement first. The only way I can describe it is what looked like a flickering flame, about two feet wide and three feet high, moving from the right side of the boiler under the water tank and proceeding into the adjoining room. I pointed it out to the team and we all watched as the flame sort of danced into the other room.

We decided to try using the divining rods again, but this time the forces moving them were much stronger than before. They were directly following our directions on who and where to point the rods, and how to move the rods to answer yes or no to our questions. There was a very short time between our questions and their answers, and the rods were moving very forcefully. None of us felt threatened or scared at any time. For me it was absolutely amazing to have the divining rods work in the way they were, and outside of an actual spirit contact, I have no explanation for why they were doing what they were doing. I seemed to have many more questions than answers as the investigation concluded. My mind was racing on the ride home with us bouncing along the road. I don't think what we experienced that night really sank in until a few days later.

LeeAnna and her team of investigators understand and examine this area from a different perspective than anyone else can. She is only beginning to comprehend the messages from the past, and it will take years for her to piece together what it is that makes Central City so haunted, what these past residents wish would happen, and why they are sticking around to make sure it does. She has the patience and compassion to accomplish these goals, and has already done a great deal to move those entities that haven't been able to rest and send them in the right direction.

My Final Ride

Following our 2012 investigation, I decided to take one more ride on the forest road between my home and Central City before winter set in, but this time I took my motorized dirt bike. As I was gliding through the trees, the smells of the pines and aspens flowing through the filter in my helmet were pleasing. There was a crystal clear, blue evening sky with the lights of the front range towns below me becoming visible just to the west over the divide. Change was obviously in the air. The wispy clouds of early fall were hanging low over the divide and the Indian peaks.

As I descended into the trees and past the Bald Mountain cemetery, it became temporarily dark as the beam from my headlight illuminated the trail ahead of me. I started to think about what this area looked like when it solely belonged to the Indians, way before the white man ever set foot on this ground. This thought set my mind on fast-forward as pictures from the past raced through my mind. It was as if I could see the transformation of this valley and canyon from what it was to what it is today. I could imagine the dreams, the triumphs, and the losses. It was always a place where one had to lose something for another to gain, and oh, how I feel for those who lost. When I shut down my bike at the cemetery above Central City, I was overwhelmed with the feeling that they are still here, begging to not be forgotten, to not let their lives be lived in vain because nobody wishes to hear their stories. Where no young person cares to learn about them, and their toils and triumphs.

A chill ran through my body as darkness fell. I had at least a ten-mile ride alone through the forest. I heard a coyote yipping out his song in the direction I would be traveling. I pushed the start button and my bike rumbled to life, breaking the silence of this wonderful place. As I turned to leave, the cemetery was behind me and I plunged back into the encompassing dark forest to the west. The thought came to me about the entire journey of my difficult life, the travels that were required to just write this book, and those whose journeys were before me, all came to light.

Maybe there is one message, just one, that all of those before us would desire to be told. That message is … "Please don't forget me …" I looked back behind me at my most favorite place in the whole world: Central City, Colorado. Its mountains, its history, and its people.

I will never forget you.

The Experts

Not all of LeeAnna Jonas's investigations have gone well. An investigation that she and her team recently conducted at an old art studio in Central City took a very bad turn for one member of her team. Like every other building in the town, this old building reportedly had a ghost or two residing there. LeeAnna and the SRIP team had long thought that there may be something very sinister going on with the spirits in Central City. A psychic even informed the team of three very evil spirits inhabiting the town.

Many times the team would be at a location doing an investigation, and it would lead to a pleasant communication with several spirits. Then the communication would suddenly stop and be replaced with a much more sinister entity. "It was as if this powerful spirit would run the other off," LeeAnna observed. "It's as if they are trying to hide something."

The Spirit Realm team supported the theory that there were three evil entities, but up until the time of this particular investigation, only two had been identified. The theory was that the three angry spirits controlled the what, where, and when of any communication with the living, and especially the investigators. It was believed that they had even attached themselves to people who were close to the investigating team to interfere with their work. The million dollar question, however, is why? What are these spirits afraid of? What do they want to hide? On this evening, it would appear that the third, and seemingly angriest, of the kingpin ghosts was ready to identify themself.

The team had a bad feeling the second they entered the building. As they walked around the lower floors of the building, the electronic voice detectors were almost immediately recorded saying "GET OUT!!" The recording also includes a member of the team joking saying the same words almost immediately following the entity saying it. This would suggest that a spirit might have some sort of subconscious control over what a human will say or do.

Only twenty minutes into the investigation, a member of the team started to experience what was a barrage of physical attacks on her body. The spirit box emitted the word "squeeze" at the very second that one of the female team assistants started to feel a mild choking sensation around her neck. It increased at an alarming rate until she almost dropped to the floor. LeeAnna stood by the assistant screaming for the spirit, or even spirits, to leave her alone. Whatever it was seemed to back off, and the team moved on to the third floor.

As the team moved to the upper floor, the name Vector became prominent in their communications. At that time, all other contacts seemed to vanish. In minutes, the attacks on the team member started again. She was being choked around her throat again and had a feeling that she describes was as if a hand was inside her abdomen, forcefully squeezing her internal organs. She remembers the pain was excruciating and that she was unable to walk. Her oxygen was gone and she was nearly incapacitated. Again, LeeAnna stood beside her to try and fight off the attack, but this time it didn't work. The team decided they needed to get her out of the building immediately. They helped her down the stairs and out to the sidewalk. It wasn't until she was outside the building that the assistant started to feel a reprieve in the attack, but she still feel very physically sick.

The camera operator drove her away from the location, and LeeAnna went back in the building to collect their equipment that had been left behind. While she was inside the building, LeeAnna started screaming at the attacker.

Suddenly, the attack turned to her. Being in the building alone, she decided to make a quick exit being fully aware that she couldn't do anything for this location. The spirit was too strong and very angry.

The assistant was taken home to her apartment in Denver and was completely wiped out from the experience, but it seemed that her frightful night wasn't quite over. While looking out of her window, she noticed a dark and transparent human figure standing in her yard, staring straight back in at her. She was understandably terrified, and frantically called LeeAnna, who then contacted a friend to come and cleanse the property. This seemed to work, but unfortunately this dark spirit seemed to move to the camera operator.

Ever since this investigation, the name Vector continually appears and ends all communication with other contacts. It also dominates and interferes will all of their investigations. Whoever or whatever this Vector is, it is not happy.

The Ghost Game

It seems that there is a strong belief among the residents in Central City that there is most definitely a persistent attempt to communicate, and most definitely a message, with those who are receptive to pass some sort of important message to further generations. Many think that it may even be a key to the town's survival.

LeeAnna Jonas is one of the strongest believers of this theory, and has personally conducted more than her fair share of investigations in this town. She is even feeling pressure now as other investigative groups are trying to push their way into the city to conduct their own investigations. Believe it or not, there is an actual ghost business, which is more of a push for notoriety, action, and thrills than in furthering scientific evidence.

LeeAnna warns, "I just hope they know what they are getting into."

I believe she is right. Doing something just to agitate and aggravate entities to increase paranormal events to gain video or audio footage is just playing with fire. These investigators do not realize that a great number of these contacts could very well be of a demonic nature, as some of these stories have proven. The point is to bring peace to those souls that are lost, hear their stories, and protect them from the people just fooling around in the ghost business that could destroy everything the SRIP team has worked toward.

Personally, I think people think this is a game. It seems similar to the interest in the late nineteenth century of the paranormal when a séance was considered as just a fun pastime. When dealing with the paranormal, it is foolish to treat it as a game, and mistakes could turn in to a lifetime of misery for those who are inexperienced and somehow get into trouble, but don't have the knowledge to get themselves out of it.

chapter six

Monsters and Things That Really Go Bump in the Night

Cryptozoology is the search and study of animals whose existence or survival is uncertain or unsubstantial, such as the Loch Ness Monster. Although this term only started to be widely used in the past few decades, the legends and stories of such creatures are ancient. They have been embedded into Native American lore and passed on from generation to generation. The accounts of some of these creatures also found their way into diaries of white trappers and explorers in the 1700s, and have continued on to today.

There was a statement made regarding cryptozoology a few years ago that perfectly demonstrates the thoughts of those who study and believe such a thing:

"Either we have been the victims of an incredible hoax that has spanned hundreds of years and more than a few generations, or there is a yet undiscovered human-like primate living in the forests of the Pacific Northwest."

Teddy Roosevelt even recalled in his book *The Wilderness Hunter* about a story that was told to him of a very violent and deadly encounter with a creature that would eventually come to be known as Bigfoot. Roosevelt's story tells of a creature that stalked two trappers, and eventually killed one of them. Today, do a quick Internet search and you can find anything you ever wanted to know, or didn't want to know, about Bigfoot. They range from scientifically based research to gimmicks of hoaxers and hecklers. The biggest issue with modern-day evidence and alleged sightings is that of credibility. Those who truly believe they have seen this mythical creature are apprehensive to come forward out of fear of being ridiculed and judged. Why would someone open themselves up to the type of scrutiny customary to the Internet-driven world? I have found that grandchildren, nieces, nephews, and other relatives of the storytellers are more inclined to talk about it.

My issue is really with the viability of pulling off a believable hoax. Although I am guilty of pulling off a Bigfoot hoax—don't get angry, it was a joke, and you will read about the story later—it didn't turn out like I thought it would, and it wasn't as easy as some may think. Taking into consideration that most sightings in Colorado have occurred at night in mines, forests, mountaintops, and in secluded areas, most people would not take the time and energy necessary to be in these exact places for a hoax to work. Consider that in order for someone to create a believable hoax, they would need to create a Bigfoot suit, trek miles into the lonely backcountry of the Rocky Mountains, suit up, and wait for who knows how long until a poor, unsuspecting hiker, just by chance, happens to walk to the very spot the person is waiting, and have them catch a glimpse of the suit out the corner of their eye. Seems to be a lot of work just for a joke. What would the payoff for something like this be?

Most of the sightings in Colorado also occur during hunting season when there are an abnormally high number of people tromping around the woods. This also doesn't seem like a good time to be dressing up like an ape and wandering around the countryside, just to scare a hunter carrying a gun. The hunter would most likely have no trouble shooting at an unknown figure. I cannot say whether Bigfoot exists or not, but I do know that one thing we need in society today is a good mystery. It's impossible for us to know everything, but life would be boring if we did! People need something to give them a good chill now and then when they look out the window late at night, or at the campground in the early morning hours.

Bigfoot "77"

My earliest encounter with Bigfoot was when I was eleven years old, and it still gives me goose bumps to think about it. Growing up, my mother always listened to the local radio station as she got ready for work every morning. The two morning DJs were fun to listen to and always had fun humor in their programs. It was a very cold winter in the Midwest that year, and a possible Bigfoot sighting on an Indian reservation in South Dakota had made the evening news, and was the topic of discussion on the radio program the following morning.

Somehow, the radio hosts decided they wanted to go see if they could track down that Bigfoot to prove it actually existed. A local car dealership in the area even got involved and offered the DJs a truck to use if they went. The DJs were committed to finding Bigfoot and made the trip to South Dakota. They broadcasted every morning on their way and reported what they were finding. The reports were humorous, but soon became more serious as the trip wore on.

It was the dead of winter, so the cold was an issue for them. In the older trucks, frost would build up on the inside of the windows, so they had to scrape them off from the inside so they could see and get pictures if the opportunity presented itself. They were able to interview a couple of witnesses, and noted that the people there believe they saw something, even if they weren't sure of exactly what it was. On the last day of their adventure, the DJs announced they were following a tracker, and thought they were getting close because they had both seen footprints in the snow.

For the first time in my life, I remember hearing a DJ recall a horrifying incident. On the last night of their adventure they described a blood-curdling scream. One of the personalities said his tape recorder had frozen up and was useless. The tone turned very serious on this last broadcast.

One of the DJs said, "Really people. I think we just got too close to it. It was a sound that made you want to go home."

I of course, was thrilled, as were some of my classmates whose parents were also listening. This just added fuel to my fire. Then came the fall of 1979 when an outbreak of alleged sightings were reported by the local media in central Iowa. A Bigfoot was spotted crossing the interstate and one was spotted in the backyard of a local residence. In addition to these, there was one more sighting, and they were all documented by the press and local law enforcement. I couldn't believe that this was happening. I thought Bigfoot was a mountain creature. How and why would it be here? And if it was here, how was it staying hidden? The phenomenon soon became much more personal.

Not Even Safe at Home

We had just moved into our house in March of 1980 on a quiet dead-end street across from my best friend. Behind our house was a portion of a cornfield, and behind that was a wire fence that surrounded what was basically a swamp. It had been used for pasture some years earlier, but at that time it was extremely overgrown with tall reeds and damp grass leading to a marsh. Storm-damaged trees lined the area and made it an inhospitable area, even though it was surrounded by subdivisions. The next house closest to ours was about a quarter of a mile away, so it was a great place for a young boy to grow up.

We had just bought a puppy, and Mom and I were not sleeping very well taking care of him. At about 1:30 one morning, my mother awoke to something walking past her bedroom window, which faced a cornfield. You could hear the cornstalks crunching under an animal that sounded like it was very heavy. My mother noticed it didn't sound like a cow, which was her first guess. She thought it sounded more like a man walking, judging by the speed that it passed by compared to how many steps it took to cover the distance. It seemed to go right past the window and straight to the side of the house toward the swamp. That's when our neighbor's two dogs started to bark and chase whatever it was that was out there, which was now walking along the fence by the swamp.

My mother went to the kitchen window that faced in that direction after turning on the back porch light to watch. The puppy woke me up, so on my way to the basement to check on him, I saw Mom at the window and, of course, had to stop. We both listened and watched for almost an hour and a half for what was going on. We could hear it walking back and forth along the fence line in very deep, dried reeds. It was as if this creature didn't know where to go.

We never saw anything, but we could guess approximately where it was by the barking dogs. They would run to our house and come into the range of our porch light, and stare at something we couldn't see. It was as if the dogs would work up the nerve and move in for an attack, and then would soon yelp and come crying back to our house, only to repeat the whole thing over again. There were even times that it sounded like both of the dogs were being hit with something. It didn't sound like a baseball bat or stick because those would make particular noises when it stuck something. This sounded like something else. The whole ordeal ended with a final attack we heard on the north side of the swamp, maybe 150 yards away.

My friend and I wanted to check the area out on our bikes, but were too scared in the days following. We finally worked up the nerve a week later to scan the fence line. We found what looked like a path that the animal took, but that was it. We reported the information to the appropriate authorities, if only to help establish a pattern for tracking purposes or to positively identify whatever was outside of our house that night, but nothing of this nature occurred in our neighborhood or in that area again that I am aware of.

However, about the same time we had our visitor, a worker at a local recreation area appeared on the news and reported seeing a tall creature next to a shelter at the park. The worker reported that the creature's head had been taller than the lowest part of the shelter's roof, which is eight feet high. To positively identify what was outside of our house that night or what was spotted at the park is impossible, but it was quite a coincidence to have this occur between the other sightings that made the news that year.

A Nervous Stop in Lake George

Hauling equipment for the logging industry is unpredictable. The jobs and locations of the operations could change daily at all hours of the day and night. A person can become somewhat use to the crazy schedules, and even crazier requests for pickups and deliveries that, almost always, seem to involve driving an eight-foot tractor-trailer on logging roads and forest access roads that normally don't see anything larger than your average pickup truck. The men who provide these services always end up sleeping in the woods at any given time, and actually prefer it. They are not the type to be afraid of the dark, and wouldn't admit it if they were.

William Boyd was dispatched from the west slope of Colorado to a logging show near Lake George in September 2009. William was thrilled about the job because it had been a few weeks since he had been in a town larger than 10,000 people, and he was looking forward to a nice supper that night. He might even hit the truck wash if he had time. He was within an hour of his destination when he got a call to stop and wait because he may be needed to turn around to move equipment to another location. This was very unwelcome news for William because it meant three or four more days in the woods, and at the least, a delay in the Lake George work. He had had his heart set on staying the night in a motel, a hot shower, and calling it an early night.

William impatiently waited, calling his dispatch now and then to try and speed up the decision about where he was going. As usual, the calls all went to voicemail because the job boss was most likely deep in the woods without cell phone service. At around 8:30 p.m., William finally received the call he had been waiting for. He was to continue on as originally planned to Lake George and head to Colorado Springs. As a consolation, the boss instructed the crew in Lake George to take the load to a yard where logs and equipment were being stored that was right on William's way to the next stop so it would be easier to load and go. The even better news was that it was a new machine that William was picking up, so there should be no mechanical issues with it. William was given the information he would need and was soon on his way.

His evening had been ruined because of the long wait, but he decided to just get it done and head on his way. It was a beautiful evening, and there was just a sliver of the moon in the sky as he turned on the brake and eased into the valley just before Lake George. Luckily, he had seen the yard where he was picking up before so he roughly knew where he was going, but it was so dark out he didn't want to miss the turn. He found the road and entrance to the yard, so he stopped the truck, got out, and tried the combination he had been given for the gate. Luckily, the combination worked. William pulled the gate open and looked into the yard, but didn't see the machine he was picking up. It was pitch-black and there were no lights on except at a church that was about a mile away.

There was a lot of older logging equipment lined along a dirt path in the yard, a large pile of logs off to the left, and some round bales of hay to the right. William climbed back into his truck and turned on all of his off-road lights, mumbling to himself about the machine being there. He slowly crept into the yard with the lights on, looking for what he was picking up. About 100 yards into the yard, he found the machine and found a good spot to turn the truck around to prepare to load. It was unbelievable how the beams of his lights didn't seem to help at all in the darkness.

He began his walk over to the machine, which was just a few yards away. The only noise was the quiet rumble of the engine in his truck, fading away as he walked into the dark to get the machine started. That was when he heard what sounded like one log hitting another. His first thought was that a log had fallen off of the pile, which sometimes happens. But the noise sounded like it came from the trees in the opposite direction of the pile he saw coming into the yard.

He started the machine and fumbled with the light switches. He decided to see if the machine's lights, shining straight where the noise came from, would help him figure out what it was. He couldn't see anything except an old rusting truck a few yards ahead of the tree line. The lights didn't do any good past that. He pulled up to his trailer and threw out some chains to tie the machine down. He kept looking over his should the whole time he was working because the unidentified noise was bothering him. All of the lights from his truck and the machine he was loading were actually making it more difficult to see the tree line. In addition to that, the noise from him throwing chains and equipment, along with the idling machines, were bothering him as well.

If something or someone were out there, they could sneak right up to him and he wouldn't be able to hear it coming.

He sped up his work and kept as much of an eye on the trees as he could. When he climbed back down to the ground, he heard what sounded like a rock hitting that old truck he saw on the tree line. This time his hair was standing up and his nostrils were flared. He stopped working and grabbed the bars on the machine, thinking he may want to jump back into the security of the steel cab. He listened for a minute, and then saw what he thought was movement at the tree line and heard a sort of grunt; kind of like what a horse would let out when it felt threatened, but with a low grumbling growl to it.

After staring for a few minutes, William realized he wanted out of there, but that meant going back out to finish securing the machine to his trailer, and that would take both noisy and labor-intensive activity that would make it difficult to watch his back. He decided to take care of his truck first so that he could make the quickest exit possible. After taking care of that, he started securing the machine on his trailer with chains, which was the noisier of the two tasks. He was walking back to the front of his trailer for more chains when he tripped over a three-foot piece of tree limb. Throughout the course of the night he had walked past that exact spot at least six times and had never seen a tree limb. He believes it was either placed or thrown there. Neither of which he would have been able to hear because of the noise he was making with the chains.

He stopped again to try and get his eyes to focus and adjust on the tree line, but this time he was holding a four-foot bar in his hands. He still couldn't see any movement at the edge of the trees, so he threw the remaining equipment on his trailer and headed out of there. He drove out of the gate slowly so he didn't cause any trouble with the partially secured load and parked on the highway next to the yard. He was in such a hurry to get out there that he even forgot to lock the gate behind him. He hurriedly tied the rest of the machine down and started his uneasy drive to his next stop.

He didn't feel any better until he came under the lights of the next town. There has been no clue as to what was out in that yard with William. But whatever it was didn't seem to like the company of a man doing his job. There have been several reports publicized in that area of wood knocking and rock throwing, and even some vocalizations. No matter what, William decided he had had enough, and has never been at ease in the woods ever since.

Hunting Alone

In 1977 my good friend, Jim, and his brother decided to take a hunting trip in the mountains in southern Colorado. They set up camp in a beautiful area, however, the weather was a bit warmer than normal for hunting. They knew if they were going to find anything, they would have to trek higher into the rugged mountains to do it. The next morning, they set out on what was sure to be a long day of searching for signs of animals nearby, and then hiking into the higher altitudes to find them. Continuing higher and higher, they soon found themselves close to the timberline.

Jokingly, Jim looked at his brother and said, "It's a good thing we brought hot dogs, cuz I haven't even seen a bird."

His brother remarked that he too thought it was strange that there was scant evidence of any living creatures in that area, outside of the tracks that they were leaving. The two men stopped and rested for a few minutes before deciding to go just a little further before turning around and heading back to camp. They walked maybe 300 yards and were at the timberline when they came to a small snowfield that lay between two rock outcroppings in a depression about 100 yards long.

The brothers said nothing to each other as they studied what appeared to be human footprints cutting across the snowfield and running the full length from one outcropping to another. Jim, who stands at more than six feet tall, noticed that for every two steps he took, the creature that left the other tracks only took one. Both brothers studied the tracks in complete silence, and then began to look around the area from where they were with an uneasy feeling. They decided to head back to camp and pack up, and head out the next morning.

After all these years, Jim still refuses to go hunting again. He never gave an indication or even tried to explain what animal or creature he thought left those tracks at that secluded, and lonely, location high in the mountains.

Just Another Evening in Park County

It was a typical evening in June 2011 for Erin, who was a teenage girl on summer break. Her biggest worry was keeping a good enough phone signal so she could continue to text her friends at a late hour. She found that if she could stay close to an open window, on one side of her house, in her third-story bedroom, she did pretty well.

While waiting for her friends to answer her messages, Erin sat next to the window. She heard what sounded like someone hitting a tree with another piece of wood in the neighbor's yard. Pine trees, with the exception of a horse corral that had been cleared out and was well-maintained, surrounded the two houses. Erin looked out of her window, but saw nothing. It seemed strange to hear that kind of noise just before midnight, but being a teenager, she decided not to give it much attention. She went back to texting her friends, but a few minutes later she heard what sounded like someone walking in the grass toward her house. It was approaching with slow, deliberate footsteps that grew louder as the intruder came closer to the house. Growing more and more frightened, Erin decided to go and tell her mother about the footsteps.

"Mom! I think something's outside!" Erin said.

"There's always something outside," her mother replied.

Erin angrily ran back up to her bedroom and turned off the light so she could get a better look at whatever was outside. This time, she not only heard it walking very slowly, one step at a time, very close to the house, but also heard very heavy breathing. It wasn't panting, but it was the type of breathing that sounded like it was coming from a very large animal, and it was probably right under her bedroom deck.

This time she thought her mom would absolutely care, so Erin ran down the stairs again and exclaimed, "Mom! I hear it breathing!"

"I have the gun. We'll be okay," was all her mother sleepily replied.

Now Erin was really mad and ran back upstairs to her bedroom window to see if she could identify the trespasser. From her bedroom window she saw a large black figure walking from under her deck toward the horse corral, and turn through a patch of tall grass. The figure was walking on two legs and was moving downhill from the house. Erin was frozen as she watched it disappear into the darkness. She finally sat down in frightened amazement at what she had just seen.

For the third time Erin went back downstairs and told her mom what she had seen. This time her mother became concerned and followed her back upstairs. But of course this time when they looked outside, there was no sign of the creature. Erin's father and brother soon came home and she ran out to tell them what she saw. The three of them searched the yard and found a narrow path cut through the grass below the house where Erin had said it had walked, but there were no footprints. The ground was soft because the path went directly over a leach field. A hoofed animal would easily have left tracks in that soil because several deer already had in that same location.

Later that summer, Erin's grandmother said she had heard a very loud and strange group of screams coming from a deep gulch just half a mile from the house. The family also had several nights where they could hear dogs barking while trailing something in the area, and then suddenly the barking would stop.

Second Rifle Season

As for many other areas that have been talked about, the flattop area of White River National Forest in Colorado has had more than its share of weird stories. For Troy Mackley and his family, however, it has been nothing more than a great place to camp and hunt. Troy and his brother were both farms boys, and everything that comes with that. Their father believed in strengthening and raising his sons through hard work and life experiences. For him, telling them what to do was only part of it. Their trips into the National Forest were no exception.

As per their father's request, both the boys would set up their own camp about half a mile away from their father's. They would cook their own supper, sleep by themselves, prepare their own breakfast, and were expected to be ready to hunt by the time they met back up with their father. Of course, their father would keep an eye on them throughout the night, but there is no better way to learn than to perform the tasks on their own.

On one such night, Troy and his brother had set up their camp, eaten supper, and were just sitting by the fire when something caught Troy's eye at the tree line just a few yards away. It was a dark and looming figure that Troy immediately associated with an elk or moose. He alerted his brother, who was siting right beside him, and they sat and watched the animal for a couple minutes.

Troy stood up and moved a little closer to the animal to get a better look because something about it seemed a bit odd. The figure he was looking at was large, but appeared to be standing on two legs instead of the four-legged animal he had expected to see. The animal seemed to be as interested in him as he was in it. Troy suddenly wished his father were with them because he was totally unable to identify what he was seeing. His brother was just as confused as he was. It would have been very difficult to run to their father's camp because the animal was directly in their path, and they didn't want to frighten off whatever this was. After a few minutes, the creature turned and walked away into the darkness of the Rocky Mountain evening. The boys toughed out the rest of the night and stayed at their camp until the morning.

The next day, Troy and his brother tried to describe what they had seen the night before to their father. As fathers do, he used a copious amount of reason and logic to describe what it was they actually saw, and the evidence in their father's mind pointed toward just a curious elk. At about mid-morning, their father spotted a bull elk backed up against a tree a few hundred yards away. The objective was to get closer to the animal so they could get a clean shot of it.

As the three guys crept closer, Troy's dad noticed that the elk wasn't moving. In fact, it looked as if it were a dog sitting up against a tree. He remarked at how strange it looked and guessed he had never seen an elk crouched like that before. They continued to slowly creep closer, and with every step Troy's father became more perplexed and confused at the elk's complete lack of concern and relaxed state at their presence. Within a few minutes and a few yards of the animal, Troy's dad decided that the animal was either sick or dead.

Cautiously moving closer, the boys and their dad saw something that made absolutely no sense. The animal was in fact dead, but still warm and crouched on its hind end in an almost grotesque way. As they drew closer to examine the animal, they noticed a small amount of steam coming from a hideous wound on the elk's chest. It looked as though the animal's chest was torn open just enough for someone or something to completely disembowel the carcass.

There was no evidence of a bullet or arrow wound on the animal, and absolutely no evidence on the ground surrounding the carcass of what surely would have been a terribly messy process of removing the animal's internal organs. Troy's dad examined the animal for a few more minutes, motioned for his sons to follow, and quickly left the area. Whether the sighting of an unidentified animal and a grotesquely disemboweled and intentionally poised and positioned elk carcass are related to each other is questionable. The Mackleys, however, knew that it was best to probably just leave it as a mystery and camp at another location.

Troy's father and uncle returned to the area the following season and had a similarly strange occurrence happen again. Once again, the men decided to leave it as a mystery and didn't investigate any further. These stories, oddly enough, are very familiar in the active area of the Colorado backcountry.

Bigfoot Hoax

My wife and I relocated to Colorado after I finished technical school and almost immediately started exploring the mountains. We wanted to see everything in our new home. We easily made a lot of new friends who shared our interests, and were able to travel every corner of the beautiful area. We would start our trips in the early evening, and would go all night without experiencing anything out of the ordinary. Then we moved into the heart of the Rocky Mountains.

In those days it was a very lonely place, especially in the winter when the summer residents go home. Access to the area was only available with an off-road vehicle after October, and we loved every minute of it. I became a member of the local fire department and was able to become well acquainted with the area and its people. When family and friends would come and visit, I noticed how uneasy they would get in these surroundings. Especially when we would take them out on four-wheelers or have a campfire late at night.

It made me realize how numb I had become to my surroundings. The bumps or noises in the dark of night did nothing to raise the hair on my neck or cause me to raise an eye to the possibility that something could be out there that is unknown to science. The great redneck hoax philosophy is that in the midst of doing something really stupid, you may learn a good lesson. It was an opportunity I couldn't pass up.

As a fire department, we had a slash pile to burn. The residents of the area who were cleaning up their yards or lots created the pile. We decided to burn the pile on a Friday evening one Labor Day weekend so our volunteers would have extra time to monitor it. We stationed our small pumper truck by the pile that was in a parking lot of an old ski area. A volunteer, Tim, came forward to spend the night with the pumper to monitor the fire so it wouldn't get out of control. My accomplice, Rob, and I were quite surprised that he volunteered. Without a doubt, Tim was the most timid guy in our crew.

The fire was well under way and calming down to a manageable size, so Rob and I went home for a short break while Tim stayed and watched the fire. Rob and I jumped on our four-wheelers and rode back to the fire and sat with Tim well into the night. It was a perfect Colorado night with clear skies and the tree line lit up by the massive pile of glowing embers. The conversation at times like this always seemed to go toward the paranormal for some reason, and Rob and I noticed that it was starting to bother Tim. We nodded to each other in an unspoken understanding and kept it up.

Trying to maintain his composure and stature as a grown man, Tim kept trying to change the subject that had started to turn to Sasquatch and sightings that were suppose to have occurred in our area. Just before midnight, with a grin I asked Tim if he was going to be at the pile all night. He affirmed that he would, but he was obviously a little spooked. Tim asked Rob and me to stay with him, but in perfect harmony we rattled off excuses about why we couldn't stay but that we would see him in the morning. As we were leaving, I made a mental list of the situation. There was a large log at the tree line, a pumper truck at one o'clock to the log, and Tim's truck was at three o'clock from the log.

Rob pulled into my driveway right behind me. As we shut off our vehicles, with a silly grin on his face Rob asked what we were going to do. This was too good of a situation to let go by. I knew Rob was thinking what I was thinking. We were going to scare the guy alone in the woods. Rob won our coin toss, so he got to put on my black coveralls and gorilla mask. It was just after midnight and deadly quiet, so we decided to walk the mile to the pile location so we didn't alert Tim that we were coming. We agreed it would be foolish to walk along the road because most people in the area owned guns, and it was a shoot first, ask questions later kind of neighborhood.

So for our safety and to maintain the element of surprise, we chose to walk through the dense forest instead. Giggling like a couple of teenagers, we proceeded into the dark forest that separated us from my house and infinite glory. After walking head-on into several trees and tripping over a couple logs, I had blood running off my nose and on to my top lip. I turned to Rob-squatch, who I assumed was still next to me, and said we had better slow down a bit because I couldn't take another blow to the head. Realigning the battered gorilla mask, Rob-squatch agreed.

Eventually, we got to the tree line with nothing more than luck that we ended up at the log at the edge of the trees, which was exactly where we wanted to be! We approached a quaint scene, lit up by the embers of the fire, our pumper truck, an empty lawn chair, and Tim's rusty truck, which is where we assumed Tim was because his boots were on the ground beside it. I directed Rob-squatch's movement to where I thought he would get the most eerie exposure to Tim's line of sight. Rob went into action like a Navy SEAL, staying to the tree line and leaving me behind to document the events.

There never was, and never will be, a better Rob-squatch. With a slumped over, apelike walk and grunting loudly, he walked into view from behind the fire and back into the trees. There was no response from Tim or the truck. Rob ran back to where he started and looked back at me from a point where Tim couldn't see him, trying so hard to hold back laughter. Rob gave me a hand gesture wondering why Tim hadn't responded to the noises. I motioned for Rob to do it again, so once again Rob-squatch was on the move, but this time he improvised. He took the same path as before, but this time he grunted louder and picked up a six-foot log and threw it into the fire, causing sparks and flames to erupt. In a very grotesque way he hobbled back into the trees. It was so good he almost scared me! Once again though, there was no response from Tim.

This time the gloves came off. Tim had to be in the back of the truck, so I told Rob to go back out there and make it really noisy this time. It was obvious we needed more than just a mysterious sighting with this guy. He must have been in a coma! This time it was pure Hollywood. Rob grunted, groaned, picked up the lawn chair next to the truck, and climaxed by throwing an even bigger tree into the fire and returned to the tree line, dropped to his knees and crawled to me so we could watch.

I was laughing so hard and could barely breath when the tailgate of the truck opened and Tim yelled, "HEY!" He bailed out of the back of the truck, jumped into the driver's seat, and floored it out of there leaving his boots, the pumper truck, and the fire to fend for themselves.

By the time Rob and I caught our breath, Tim had squealed to a stop at the bottom of my driveway, run the eighty feet up the driveway with his socks half off of his feet to the door, and pounded on the door until my wife answered. Tim was screaming and asking her where I was and telling her there was a drunken man raiding his camp. In on the act, my wife tried to hold it back, but she burst out laughing. She then explained to him exactly who the person really was terrorizing the camp. As Rob-squatch and I hobbled back through the dark woods and arrived at my house around 1:30 a.m., full of pride at the havoc we had just created, we had no idea until the next morning how close the joke had come to backfiring on us, in a very serious way.

My neighbor, Ron, who lived just down the road awakened me early the next morning. He was carrying his rifle and didn't even give me time to talk. He pulled me behind my storage shed, which was eight feet from the patio that Rob and I were yukking it up on just less than five hours before. There was a large pool of blood with air bubbles in it that was maybe ten inches in diameter. Confused at what this was, Ron explained that at about 1:15 that morning, another neighbor who lived just up the hill had watched a 220-pound bear, who was bleeding, leave his deck. Hearing about the incident, Ron tracked the blood trail to my house. I stood there for a second letting it sink in as the timeline started to come together. I asked him if he had called the division of wildlife, and he said they were en route and we should put it down if we saw it. I was silent for a few seconds, trying to digest the information.

I went into the house to get my rifle. I didn't relish the thought of shooting a bear, but thought if it was still alive, it must be hurting. I started at my neighbor's house where the bear was first sighted and followed a scant blood trail to my house, which was all downhill. The bear had obviously moved very quickly to my house and then stayed there behind my shed for quite awhile before proceeding to the creek below. The blood trail told me that somewhere in the pitch-black morning hours, Rob-squatch and I crossed paths with a mortally wounded black bear. With my knowledge of wounded bears, I became very frightened as we tracked down the poor animal's last steeps into the creek. We continued to follow a scant blood trail, but the bear was never found either by the wildlife officers or us. He got away from us and vanished with at least two experienced trackers following him.

In addition to that, Tim did start to speak to Rob and me again after a few weeks. It was a slow process, but we soon found common ground to communicate.

There are several points that must be noted from this story. To execute a Bigfoot hoax is ludicrous at best. Someone who had just had Sasquatch stories pounded into his head just hours before misidentified us. It should have been fresh on his mind. This story is just a shred of evidence in favor of the fact that a very large animal can very effectively hide from humans even if it is in distress. Our senses are numb compared to other mammals. A dog would have detected that bear, but we couldn't from less than ten feet away.

Epilogue

Writing this book has truly been an adventure. I discovered stories from my childhood that were held in some sort of memory bank that were just waiting to come out. It has been a work in progress, taking a large chunk of my life, and with chance meetings with hundreds of people willing to tell me their stories. I am so fortunate and thankful for the experiences I have had in my active life.

While compiling stories for a book like this, one would want to search for answers. I am afraid, however, that I have come up with more questions. One conclusion I have come to is that we as humans still really don't have a clue about anything. Most of us seem trapped in our own realities without being able to take a second to know our surroundings or ourselves.

I have realized that the messages from the past are simple. They want us to remember to not forget who you are and where you come from. It is really easy, but pretty hard to figure out where we are going if we don't know where we have been. There is probably a very good reason why we are where we are today, and the answers are most likely in your ancestry. Imagine trying to teach your children a lesson, but they won't listen no matter how many times you repeat it. The evidence I have recovered from my research indicates that this is the same scenario when thinking about communication from those that have passed.

I witnessed the death of a very good man who had a beautiful family, only to have his family destroyed by his widow's new husband only three years later. The contacts made to close family members were astounding. They indicated misery and abuse, which was the exact opposite of the image the family portrayed to other family and relatives. One particularly sensitive relative tried to relay to the family that she knew something was wrong, but that eventually led to losing contact with the family for many years ... until the truth came out.

I have been told there have been contacts with family members relaying accurate death predictions, dream communication of new babies who were on their way in my own family, an unhappy spirit of a mother who knew her son married the wrong woman, and several contacts warning of impending danger. In my opinion, these are most definitely more than just coincidences. The question is, will any of us ever find the time to harness these energies and try to use them to our advantage?

I hope so. We have gotten too fast for ourselves, to the point that we have not time to concentrate on what is really important in life. If you can hear messages, I suggest listening to them.

To Write to the Author

If you wish to contact the author or would like more information about this book, please write to the author in care of Llewellyn Worldwide Ltd. and we will forward your request. Both the author and publisher appreciate hearing from you and learning of your enjoyment of this book and how it has helped you. Llewellyn Worldwide Ltd. cannot guarantee that every letter written to the author can be answered, but all will be forwarded. Please write to:

Gary Gillespie
℅ Llewellyn Worldwide
2143 Wooddale Drive
Woodbury, MN 55125-2989, U.S.A.

Please enclose a self-addressed stamped envelope for reply, or $1.00 to cover costs. If outside the U.S.A., enclose an international postal reply coupon.

GET MORE AT LLEWELLYN.COM

Visit us online to browse hundreds of our books and decks, plus sign up to receive our e-newsletters and exclusive online offers.

- Free tarot readings • Spell-a-Day • Moon phases
- Recipes, spells, and tips • Blogs • Encyclopedia
- Author interviews, articles, and upcoming events

GET SOCIAL WITH LLEWELLYN

Find us on

www.Facebook.com/LlewellynBooks

Follow us on
twitter
www.Twitter.com/Llewellynbooks

GET BOOKS AT LLEWELLYN

LLEWELLYN ORDERING INFORMATION

Order online: Visit our website at www.llewellyn.com to select your books and place an order on our secure server.

Order by phone:
- Call toll free within the U.S. at 1-877-NEW-WRLD (1-877-639-9753)
- Call toll free within Canada at 1-866-NEW-WRLD (1-866-639-9753)
- We accept VISA, MasterCard, and American Express

Order by mail:
Send the full price of your order (MN residents add 6.875% sales tax) in U.S. funds, plus postage and handling to: Llewellyn Worldwide, 2143 Wooddale Drive Woodbury, MN 55125-2989

POSTAGE AND HANDLING

STANDARD (U.S. & Canada):
(Please allow 12 business days)
$25.00 and under, add $4.00.
$25.01 and over, FREE SHIPPING.

INTERNATIONAL ORDERS (airmail only):
$16.00 for one book, plus $3.00 for each additional book.

Visit us online for more shipping options. Prices subject to change.

FREE CATALOG!

To order, call
1-877-
NEW-WRLD
ext. 8236
or visit our
website

Marcus F. Griffin

Foreword by Jeff Belanger

EXTREME PARANORMAL

I N V E S T I G A T I O N S

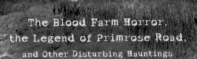

The Blood Farm Horror,
the Legend of Primrose Road,
and Other Disturbing Hauntings

Extreme Paranormal Investigations
The Blood Farm Horror, the Legend of Primrose Road, and Other Disturbing Hauntings
MARCUS F. GRIFFIN

Foreword by Ghostvillage.com founder
and author Jeff Belanger

Set foot inside the bone-chilling, dangerous, and sometimes downright terrifying world of extreme paranormal investigations. Join Marcus F. Griffin, Wiccan priest and founder of Witches in Search of the Paranormal (WISP), as he and his team explore the Midwest's most haunted properties. These investigations include the creepiest-of-the creepy cases WISP has tackled over the years, many of them in locations that had never before been investigated. These true-case files include investigations of Okie Pinokie and the Demon Pillar Pigs, the Ghost Children of Munchkinland Cemetery, and the Legend of Primrose Road. Readers will also get an inside glimpse of previously inaccessible places, such as the former Jeffrey Dahmer property as WISP searches for the notorious serial killer's spirit, and the farm that belonged to Belle Gunness, America's first female serial killer and the perpetrator of the Blood Farm Horror.

978-0-7387-2697-7, 264 pp., 5³⁄₁₆ x 8   **$15.95**

To order, call 1-877-NEW-WRLD
Prices subject to change without notice
Order at Llewellyn.com 24 hours a day, 7 days a week!

FILES
FROM THE
EDGE

A PARANORMAL
INVESTIGATOR'S
EXPLORATIONS
INTO HIGH
STRANGENESS

PHILIP J. IMBROGNO

Files From the Edge
A Paranormal Investigator's Explorations into High Strangeness
PHILIP J. IMBROGNO

Ghost lights, otherworldly creatures, visits from another dimension. The most bizarre and amazing case studies from a renowned paranormal investigator are presented here.

In his thirty-year career, Philip J. Imbrogno has researched a vast array of fascinating supernatural phenomena—the perpetually haunted mines of Putnam County, New York; encounters with strange entities at sacred megalithic stones; Bigfoot, yeti, and other humanoids; sea creatures; psychic phenomena; the dangerous Jinn; and a vast array of life forms from other worlds. The author's objective, scientific analysis—combined with credible witness testimonials and Imbrogno's own thrilling experiences—provides eye-opening, convincing evidence of our multidimensional universe.

978-0-7387-1881-1, 336 pp., 5³⁄₁₆ x 8   **$17.95**

GHOSTLY TALES OF MUSICAL LEGENDS

HAUNTED
ROCK &
ROLL

MATTHEW L. SWAYNE

Haunted Rock & Roll
Ghostly Tales of Musical Legends
MATTHEW L. SWAYNE

From rock and roll's pioneers to its contemporary rebels, explore how the greatest names live on after death—in unexpected and frightening ways. Combining two of America's great passions, celebrities and the paranormal, *Haunted Rock & Roll* covers rock's entire supernatural history.

Explore rock and roll's most iconic idols, haunted locations, and infamous legends through evidence and testimonials from renowned ghost hunters and researchers. Discover thrilling stories of Michael Jackson, Jim Morrison, Led Zeppelin, the Beatles, Amy Winehouse, and many more stars seen haunting their favorite bars, clubs, and homes. From the early days through the present pop music era, rockers have followed the same motto: Live fast, die young, and leave a restless spirit.

978-0-7387-3923-6, 288 pp, 5³⁄₁₆ x 8   **$15.99**

JAMIE DAVIS
WITH SAMUEL QUEEN

INSIDE ABANDONED
INSTITUTIONS
FOR THE CRAZY,
CRIMINAL & QUARANTINED

HAUNTED
ASYLUMS, PRISONS,
AND
SANATORIUMS

Haunted Asylums, Prisons, and Sanatoriums
Inside Abandoned Institutions for the Crazy, Criminal & Quarantined
JAMIE DAVIS

A chill runs through the air inside the Death Tunnel at Waverly Hills Hospital. The Shadow Man haunts cellblocks at the West Virginia Penitentiary. A Civil War soldier's ghost communicates through flashlights at the Trans-Allegheny Lunatic Asylum. Explore dozens of chilling ghost stories like these and 57 terrifying photographs from ten well-known, haunted institutions across the United States.

Haunted Asylums, Prisons, and Sanatoriums includes the history of each building, personal paranormal experiences from the author and facility staff, and spooky highlights from on-site tours. This spine-tingling, one-of-a-kind guide is filled with photos, historical knowledge, interviews, and frightening, first-hand stories. Readers will also enjoy an introduction to basic ghost hunting equipment and detailed information about organizing their own visits to these haunted institutions.

978-0-7387-3750-8, 240 pp., 6 x 9   **$15.99**

True Casefiles of a Paranormal Investigator
STEPHEN LANCASTER

As a ghost hunter for nearly fifteen years, Stephen Lancaster's encounters with the paranormal range from the merely incredible to the downright terrifying. This gripping collection of true casefiles takes us behind the scenes of his most fascinating paranormal investigations. See what it's like to come face to face with an unearthly glowing woman in a dark cemetery, be attacked by invisible entities, talk to spirits using a flashlight, and dodge objects launched by a poltergeist.

Every delicious detail is documented: the history and legends of each haunted location, what Stephen's thinking and feeling throughout each unimaginable encounter, and how he manages to capture ghost faces, spirit voices, a cowboy shadow man, otherworldly orbs, a music-loving spirit playing an antique piano, and other extraordinary paranormal evidence.

978-0-7387-3220-6, 240 pp., 5³⁄₁₆ x 8   **$15.95**
